WILLIAMS-SONOMA

SAN FRANCISCO

AUTHENTIC RECIPES CELEBRATING THE FOODS OF THE WORLD

Recipes and Text
JANET FLETCHER

Photographs
JEAN-BLAISE HALL

General Editor
CHUCK WILLIAMS

Oxmoor
House®

CONTENTS

RECIPES

INTRODUCTION

Where do you find real San Francisco cooking? In the taquerías of the Mission? The noodle shops of Chinatown? The sleek restaurants of SoMa? All embracing and always curious, San Franciscans today are the spiritual heirs of the city's immigrant entrepreneurs and rough-and-ready miners of 150 years ago.

CULINARY HISTORY

Two years before gold was discovered in California in 1849, San Francisco had fewer than five hundred residents. By 1850, it had thirty thousand, many of them single men. Not surprisingly, a wave of saloons, boarding-houses, and restaurants soon followed—among them, Tadich Grill, opened in 1849 (under another name) and still operating today. Within twenty years, San Francisco had a reputation as a food lover's town. Alexandre Dumas, the French gastronomic chronicler, wrote in 1873 that the city was second only to Paris in the number of its restaurants and expressed astonishment at those restaurants' ethnic diversity. In addition to its renowned French restaurants, such as the Poodle Dog, the San Francisco of the 1880s could claim eating establishments run by Germans, Croatians, Italians, and Chinese.

San Francisco boasts several restaurants that have passed the century mark: the Old Clam House (1861), Jack's (1864; which is now known as Jeanty at Jack's), Sam's Grill (1867), Fior d'Italia (1886), and Schroeder's Café (1893), along with Tadich.

The period between the world wars saw the birth of many North Beach Italian restaurants, such as Amelio's and Vanessi's. New Joe's on Broadway, originally a cover for an illicit card room in the back, became famous for its onion-topped burgers in hollowed-out sourdough bread. All three are gone now, but they were long-lived establishments that helped cement the neighborhood's reputation as a vibrant West Coast Little Italy.

Ernie's, San Francisco's most elegant restaurant for decades, also dates from the 1930s. So does Trader Vic's, a Polynesian-themed establishment opened in Oakland in 1936 by South Seas traveler Trader Vic Bergeron. The canny restaurateur, who introduced the *mai tai* and other Polynesian-style drinks that were garnished with paper umbrellas, had so many San Francisco customers that he opened another Trader Vic's in the city in 1951. For many years, the Captain's Cabin at Trader Vic's was San Francisco society's private dining room. Both Ernie's and Trader Vic's closed in the 1990s, victims of changing tastes.

René Verdon, the White House chef for John and Jacqueline Kennedy, moved to San Francisco soon after the president's death, opened Le Trianon restaurant, and ushered in a fashion for French food. Le Trianon, La Bourgogne, Ernie's, and Fleur de Lys, all luxe establishments, were the epitome of fine San Francisco dining in the 1970s.

At the other end of the dining spectrum, family-style Basque restaurants on Broadway delighted budget-conscious diners with multicourse meals and enormous servings enjoyed at communal tables. Several of these businesses had indeed been hostelries and boardinghouses for the many Basque shepherds who at one time worked on California and Nevada ranches, but as that population dwindled, the hotels changed course and opened their humble dining rooms to locals. Meals almost always began with a bottomless tureen of vegetable soup, to fill diners up before the first meat course.

In 1971, a young American woman introduced the Bay Area to a different side of French cooking. At Chez Panisse, Alice

Waters's revolutionary Berkeley restaurant, simplicity and flavor triumphed over pomp and ceremony. Waters's obsession with good ingredients and seasonality remain hallmarks of Bay Area cooking today, in part because so many of her former employees have taken these ideas with them to new establishments.

The 1980s saw an influx of Southeast Asians in the Bay Area and a corresponding expansion of interest in the flavors and culinary techniques of Vietnam, Thailand, Cambodia, Laos, and Burma. Modest restaurants featuring these cuisines began to surface in many neighborhoods, especially in the more affordable Richmond and Sunset districts,

and San Franciscans quickly embraced them. By the late 1980s, Asian ingredients, from galangal root to tamarind, began to appear on non-Asian menus, producing some uneasy alliances often referred to as fusion food.

As the twentieth century drew to a close, the San Francisco Bay Area—like all of California—could claim a growing Hispanic population. Mexican, Salvadoran, Nicaraguan, and Peruvian immigrants enriched Northern California's culinary scene with new markets and restaurants, encouraging Bay Area residents to stir yet more ingredients and flavors into their ever-evolving—and often inventive—local cuisine.

CONTEMPORARY CUISINE

No other American city can rival San Francisco's reputation as a serious food town. Its residents will stand in line for thirty minutes for a favorite bread, drive across town for the best coffee beans, and stretch their budget to buy locally raised grass-fed beef and organic, free-range poultry.

The contemporary Bay Area food scene has so much influence nationwide that it can be hard to discern what is truly unique about it. The region is too widely watched and imitated to keep anything to itself for long. But although chefs around the country have embraced many tenets of Northern California cuisine—freshness, seasonality, and simplicity among them—one could argue that Bay Area cooks are still the most passionate practitioners. An allegience to market-based cooking may be widespread now, but the Bay Area remains the mother church, as the wealth of local farmers' markets and other specialty outlets illustrates.

California Cuisine

The principles associated with California cuisine coalesced in the Bay Area, and although many local chefs dislike that overused phrase, it does suggest a distinctive style of cooking that still characterizes their kitchens. Among its hallmarks:

Seasonality—Menus change frequently, even daily, to reflect the seasonal availability of fresh produce and fish. Chefs showcase ingredients during their local season—asparagus in spring, wild salmon in summer, blood oranges in winter—then take them off the menu, rather than use seafood or produce shipped from afar.

An appreciation for vegetables—Fresh vegetables get star treatment on many Bay Area main-course plates. They are not an afterthought. At contemporary restaurants like Boulevard in San Francisco, the creative vegetable preparations enliven main-course compositions, and many diners choose their centerpiece based on the allure of the "sides" (side dishes). Some chefs highlight side dishes in a separate category and don't object if diners make a meal of them.

A love affair with the grill—The aroma of charcoal has infused Bay Area cooking since the early 1980s, with the debut of San Francisco's Hayes Street Grill and Berkeley's Fourth Street Grill, the latter gone now. Today, a charcoal grill is standard restaurant equipment, and diners expect that their burgers, steaks, fish, and chicken will be grilled over live coals, not gas. The Bay Area predilection for live-fire cooking extends to baking as well. In several Bay Area restaurants, wood-fired ovens turn out flame-licked pizza and calzone. And some of the most-admired local breads—including the handsome, high-priced loaves produced by Della Fattoria—come from wood-burning ovens.

A Mediterranean spirit—Dishes inspired by or directly borrowed from Provence, Italy, and Spain dominate so many Bay Area menus that diners sometimes forget that these preparations are foreign. Aioli, polenta, focaccia, and crostini have been absorbed into the local vocabulary, and virtually every restaurant goer knows how to pronounce pancetta, radicchio, and *bruschetta.*

A passion for quality—The best Bay Area chefs share a deeply held belief that good cooking depends on good raw materials. They go out of their way to secure produce, eggs, meat, and poultry directly from the producers and critically examine their own choices of everything from olive oil to salt. Many home cooks, taking a cue from the chefs, are equally discriminating and willingly pay a premium for artisanal pasta, cheese, or bread. Several specialty-food stores and carriage-trade markets service this demanding clientele, and their popularity underscores the Bay Area philosophy that good ingredients matter.

A taste for simplicity—Diners elsewhere may fall for highly embellished food, towering architectural presentations, or elaborate and fussy garnishes, but Bay Area chefs and diners have simpler tastes. Flavor matters more than form on local restaurant plates, and customers are not seduced by food that looks better than it tastes. Complex sauces have lost favor in Bay Area kitchens, replaced by techniques, such as searing and braising, that heighten intrinsic flavors. A spit-roasted organic chicken rubbed with herbs or an impeccably fresh fillet of grilled halibut drizzled with Meyer lemon vinaigrette appeals to local tastes more than fancier, flashier dishes.

An international pantry—Bay Area chefs draw inspiration from dozens of cultures and enjoy using traditional ingredients in nontraditional ways. For many, the world is their pantry. Vietnamese fish sauce sparks their Caesar salad or steak tartare. Balsamic vinegar adds resonance to their barbecue

sauce. Thai curry paste and coconut milk cloak the local king salmon, and wasabi invigorates a slaw. Although some chefs are more comfortable staying within a relatively pure Mediterranean idiom, others open their Bay Area kitchens to almost any immigrant ingredient, from Southeast Asian lemongrass and kaffir lime leaves to Mexican chorizo and Peruvian chiles.

A concern for sustainability—The Bay Area's reputation for environmentalism and left-leaning politics extends to its food choices. Many chefs and consumers seek out organic produce, avoid seafood reported to be over-fished, and buy only from meat and poultry suppliers that practice humane animal husbandry. Although such activist shoppers are surely in the minority, they have had a pronounced impact on local food options. Many Bay Area supermarkets give substantial space to organic produce and sell naturally raised pork and organic chicken. A few markets, like some local restaurants, offer the more environmentally friendly grass-fed beef.

In growing numbers, Bay Area chefs and consumers see eating as a political act.

Vegetarian Influences

The Bay Area's many vegans, vegetarians, and almost-vegetarians shape the menus at local restaurants and food shops. Most restaurants offer at least one meatless main course and willingly accommodate special requests from meat avoiders.

So often in the vanguard, Bay Area diners have also helped popularize one of the more curious modern culinary movements: the art of not cooking. Raw food, believed by some to be more healthful than cooked food, has many adherents in the Bay Area, and a critically acclaimed vegetarian restaurant, Roxanne's in Larkspur, is devoted to that philosophy.

Dining at Home

When dining at home, Bay Area residents have remarkably multicultural tastes, thanks to the ethnically diverse food they encounter in restaurants. Bay Area supermarkets, with

their vast prepared-food selections, offer good clues to what locals eat for dinner. Rotisserie chicken and roasted vegetables go home with those with play-it-safe tendencies. Others fill their shopping carts with sesame noodles, sushi, vegetarian tamales, or *pad Thai* (stir-fried Thai noodles). And, of course, some people still do cook at home. At the enormous, frenetic 99 Ranch Markets (in Richmond, Daly City, and elsewhere), which stock virtually everything for the Asian cook, shoppers are three-deep at the phenomenal seafood and meat counters, buying whole fish, head-on shrimp, live crabs, and fresh chickens with feet attached.

Thanks to the Bay Area's mild weather, outdoor cooking is virtually a year-round sport. Cooks elsewhere may be content to grill burgers, steaks, and chicken, but the Bay Area's amateur chefs believe that just about any food likes a live fire. These fearless grillers sear squid, asparagus, radicchio, carrots, artichokes, and figs. Their ovens may not get a workout, but their grills never rest.

DINING OUT

In San Francisco, restaurant debuts and demises and the comings and goings of celebrity chefs fill newpaper gossip columns, and the city's top food critic has power to rival the mayor's. Residents consider dining out a competitive sport, and Monday morning office conversations center on who ate where over the weekend.

With more than 3,300 table-service restaurants, San Francisco offers enough dining possibilities to keep local restaurant enthusiasts on the move. And although it would be difficult to prove, San Franciscans certainly believe that they have the country's most ethnically diverse restaurant inventory. Bay Area food aficionados can start the day with a *pain au chocolat* at Tartine, grab a stand-up lunch at a taco truck on Oakland's International Boulevard, and wind up the evening at Aziza, feasting on refined and modernized Moroccan fare.

Hungry for Korean *kalbi* (short ribs) or Lebanese *fattoush* (bread salad)? San Francisco can satisfy the craving. The city seems to have at least one of every imaginable kind of dining-out venue, from old-fashioned doughnut shops to high-fashion Italian cafés; from Chinese *jook* (rice porridge) joints in Chinatown to the elegant, Hong Kong–style Harbor Village; from modest Cambodian and Burmese establishments in the Richmond and Sunset neighborhoods to swank white-tablecloth restaurants downtown.

Hallmarks of the Bay Area Table

National restaurant chains typically do poorly in San Francisco because locals shun predictability. As culinary adventurers, most San Franciscans dislike cookie-cutter experiences. For the Bay Area food enthusiast, every meal is a potential discovery.

Nevertheless, locals face the same time constraints as other Americans these days, and the typical Bay Area breakfast is often a mobile one. For commuters, as many Northern Californians are, a smoothie picked up at a juice bar or a latte and muffin from a neighborhood café may be all that tides them over until lunch.

Midday meals in the Bay Area are likely to have an ethnic bent, as people stream out of their workplaces and into quick-service restaurants for Thai green curry prawns, *carnitas* (fried pork) tacos, Japanese soba noodles, or Italian *panini* (sandwiches). Even at the large corporate campuses in Silicon Valley, where workers rarely leave for lunch, in-house cafés offer a remarkable variety of ethnic food such as chicken mole, salsa bars, and stir-fry stations.

For evenings out, San Franciscans have enough choices to satisfy any whim. In the mood for an ethnic experience, they might head to Kokkari for Greek *mezethes* (appetizers), to B44 for paella, to Fina Estampa for Peruvian *anticuchos* (skewered beef heart), or to Straits Cafe for Singaporean satay. At One Market, they can sample sophisticated California cooking; at Delfina, they can imagine themselves in Italy. Eager to try many tastes, Bay Area diners love small plates, inspired by Spanish tapas: César in Berkeley, Fonda Solana in Albany, and À Côté in Oakland are three favorites.

Restaurants That Set the Pace

For food-industry trend watchers, the Bay Area is the promised land. Many of the ideas and fashions that eventually sweep the country have their origins in restaurants here. New York City may be larger and Los Angeles more hip, but Bay Area chefs seem to have more influence on the nation's future table. Many national food companies send their creative teams to San Francisco to eat in the local restaurants and look for cutting-edge ideas.

Among the restaurants that set the pace, both locally and nationally, Chez Panisse surely leads the pack. For more than thirty years, other food professionals have looked to this Berkeley restaurant for inspiration. Buying direct from growers and ranchers, and working closely with them on quality issues, is commonplace for chefs now, but it wasn't when Chez Panisse first undertook these efforts. Chez Panisse has also led the way in its commitment to sustainable agriculture and humane animal husbandry, an example that many other chefs have followed.

On the aesthetic front, Chez Panisse introduced the notion that impeccable ingredients can trump fussy technique. Two alumni of the restaurant, Judy Rodgers at Zuni Café in San Francisco and Paul Bertolli at Oliveto in Oakland, have adhered to this notion as they introduce customers to Italian country cooking. While Bertolli is an Italian purist, Rodgers's food bears a California stamp. Many would point to Zuni Café as the most San Franciscan of local restaurants.

Of course, Thomas Keller's indisputable genius has made the French Laundry in Yountville a destination. He is a chef's chef, one whose considerable technique inspires awe and admiration. Working at a similarly ambitious level but with seafood, the chefs at Aqua and Farallon in San Francisco have restored the city's primacy as a seafood town. Other top destinations for fine dining include Gary Danko; the elegant Fleur de Lys; Traci Des Jardins' Jardiniere, popular among opera and symphony patrons; and Boulevard, the showcase for Nancy Oakes' cooking. On a

more casual note, the whimsical Fog City Diner proved that the old-fashioned diner could be updated for contemporary tastes.

Immigrant chefs such as the Vietnam-born Charles Phan at Slanted Door and the Peruvian Martin Castillo at Limón continue to stimulate local palates and to expand the definition of San Francisco food. At the perpetually busy Slanted Door, Phan has proved that diners welcome an upscale take on Vietnamese food and that his country's cooking can partner happily with wine. When he opened Limón in 2002, Castillo found an immediate and enthusiastic audience for his fresh, tingling Peruvian ceviches, yet more proof that the local palate loves a challenge.

In Inverness, a sleepy town about one hour north of San Francisco, Margaret Grade has created what many chefs dream of: a small country inn and restaurant with a menu based largely on local, seasonal foods. Manka's Inverness Lodge, her establishment, is so highly regarded that Thomas Keller has dined there on his birthday.

1509
HYDE ST. SEAFOOD HOUSE
1509
EST. 1985
OYSTERS·CLAMS·MUSSELS·FISH·
JACKSON

MARKETS

Like an old-time village square, farmers' markets bring neighbors together to share gossip and news. For many, a trip to the market is an excuse for a weekly family outing or breakfast with friends. For others, it is the best way to stock their kitchens with the finest fruits and vegetables the area has to offer.

Chief among the factors contributing to the Bay Area's dynamic food scene is the proliferation of farmers' markets. Common in European villages and cities for centuries, these lively, multivendor marketplaces had withered in the United States with the rise of the efficient, one-stop supermarket. By the 1970s, California had only about twenty farmers' markets remaining.

The decline reversed itself in the early 1980s, when community activists began organizing farmers' markets as a way to bring life to depressed urban centers and to support small farms trying to survive on the urban edge. Suburban communities around San Francisco, Oakland, and San Jose had mushroomed after World War II, chewing up farmland at an alarming rate. Once chefs and consumers began to grasp that urban-edge farms were an endangered species, the stage was set for a farmers' market revival.

Today, more than four hundred California communities have state-certified farmers' markets, and the Bay Area has more than its share. Almost every Bay Area town of any size has a weekly farmers' market, and some, like San Francisco, have several. To earn certification, the markets must admit only farmers who grow their own produce— no wholesalers or middlemen allowed.

For many of Northern California's small family farms, such markets are key to survival. The farmers get retail price for their harvest and have access to a dream audience: sophisticated shoppers willing to pay for quality and eager to try the unfamiliar. In return, the farmers offer produce that is picked vine- or tree-ripe, often the day before—a taste experience not available to the supermarket shopper. Some farmers use the market as a low-risk testing ground, a place to try out new varieties with modest investment. A few rows of unusual radishes or melons won't yield enough to interest a distributor but will provide enough to gauge consumer demand.

These much-loved markets have become more than just a place to buy peak-season produce. Parents bring children to the market to remind them that food comes from a farm, not a can; to spur their interest in eating fresh fruits and vegetables; and to awaken their senses to the pleasures of a vine-ripe tomato or tree-ripened peach. Farmers and customers share recipes at the market, and home gardeners pump growers for advice.

Bay Area farmers' markets have become such popular gathering spots that many have areas dedicated to coffee and pastry or other prepared foods to enjoy on the spot. About an hour and a half northeast of San Francisco, the town of Davis, home to one the state's oldest and most successful markets, holds a Wednesday evening summer market that draws hundreds of families who come to shop and picnic, choosing their dinner from one of several international food vendors.

Each market has its own personality, based on the neighborhood and its patrons. Oakland's Friday morning market on the edge of Chinatown draws a largely Asian clientele and many vendors offering Asian produce. Berkeley's downtown Tuesday and Saturday markets are primarily organic, a reflection of community preferences. The twice-weekly Marin Civic Center market, another long-established market with a committed clientele, features many flower and craft vendors.

In the Napa Valley, the small but delightful St. Helena morning market launches Fridays in spring and summer. Against a backdrop of grapevines and the scenic Mayacamas Mountains, weekend tourists mix with world-famous vintners, who fill their bags with goat cheese made nearby, farm-fresh eggs, and the local Long Meadow Ranch olive oil.

One of the liveliest and most riveting markets is the Alemany market on the southern edge of San Francisco. Patronized by a remarkable variety of ethnic groups, including many Indians, Southeast Asians,

Filipinos, and Hispanics, the market vividly conveys the rich cultural tapestry that is San Francisco. At Alemany, shopping bags are filled with taro root, sugarcane, *rau ram* (Vietnamese coriander), sweet potato greens, duck eggs, and lemongrass.

But surely the most influential market is the Ferry Plaza Farmers' Market on San Francisco's waterfront. On Saturday mornings, top Bay Area chefs and food professionals roam the aisles alongside passionate local foodies; Alice Waters may be spotted here, doing personal shopping from some of the same farmers who deliver to her restaurant.

Northern California's finest produce flows to this picturesque market. Summer brings the increasingly rare Blenheim apricots, plump olallieberries, and figs oozing liquid sugar. In August, Bay Area farmers' markets are about the only place to find the local Gravenstein apples, prized for applesauce but too short-lived to interest most supermarkets. In autumn, farmers hawk Brussels sprouts on the stalk, fresh cranberry beans, regal Comice pears,

and fragrant heirloom apples. Stan Devoto, who grows dozens of apple varieties at his Sebastopol farm, brings his precious harvest to Bay Area markets, tempting shoppers with tastes of Arkansas Black, Pink Pearl, Mutsu, and Spitzenburg apples, the last said to be Thomas Jefferson's favorite. Although some growers take the winter off, others fill their booths with a cornucopia of citrus, root vegetables, all manner of sturdy greens for cooking, and exquisite chicories for salads. Shoppers at the Ferry Plaza and the Marin farmers' markets know to seek out the Star Route Farm stand for cool-weather crops like broccoli rabe, arugula (rocket), Tuscan kale, nettles—a chef favorite for flavoring pasta dough—and frisée. In spring, local peas, asparagus, fava (broad) beans, and baby beets lure shoppers in droves. Growers from Pescadero and Half Moon Bay, both south of San Francisco, steal the limelight in March and April with mountains of firm, meaty artichokes ranging from as small as a walnut to softball size.

FLAVORS OF THE NEIGHBORHOODS

To know San Francisco's character, you should walk its streets, stopping occasionally for a taco or bowl of *pho*. Discover the scents of its many neighborhoods—small, discrete worlds with their own flavor and pace, and in some cases, their own language.

More than most American cities, San Francisco has distinct neighborhoods with well-known names, unwritten but understood borders, and pronounced personalities. A handful of neighboring Bay Area regions also have identifiable characters shaped by the history, landscape, merchants, and residents who define everyday life there.

The Mission

Long a largely Hispanic neighborhood filled with taquerías, *panaderías* (bakeries), and well-stocked Mexican markets like Casa Lucas, the Mission is in transition. Attracted by relatively low rents, restaurants such as the creperie Ti Couz, the Mediterranean-inspired Foreign Cinema, and the hip Peruvian Limón have moved in, making the Mission now a choice venue for chefs with cutting-edge ideas. Yet the Mission remains the destination for cooks seeking Hispanic ingredients or the tastiest *carnitas* tacos, and there are no signs that the area is losing its Latin accent.

Chinatown

Savvy food lovers come to Chinatown for the freshest fish, chickens, game birds, and duck. The jammed sidewalks and crowded shops require customers to plunge in; he who hesitates may be elbowed aside by a shopper on a mission. San Franciscans consider Chinatown a rich resource for woks and cleavers, fancy tea, dim sum, and medicinal herbs to cure every ill.

North Beach

With Columbus Avenue as its backbone and Washington Square as its heart, North Beach remains San Francisco's most Italian-accented district. Locals and tourists pack its cafés, nursing cappuccino or Campari and soda. In old-world style, shoppers make the rounds of its small food merchants, picking up focaccia at Liguria Bakery, *soppressata* at Molinari, coffee at Graffeo, biscotti at Danilo, and veal at Little City. The neighborhood houses one of the city's oldest restaurants (Fior d'Italia) and some of its most loved, including Tommaso's, a favorite for wood-oven pizza; the petite L'Osteria del Forno for simple, home-style Italian cooking; and the bustling Rose Pistola.

The Marina and Cow Hollow

One of the most desirable areas for young singles to live, the Marina and Cow Hollow neighborhoods serve their residents with lively bars (Perry's and Balboa Café, among others) and noisy, youthful restaurants like Betelnut and Café Marimba. Chestnut, Union, and Fillmore Streets are perpetually packed with twenty-something shoppers. Those with a culinary bent patronize Fredericksen Hardware for cookware and casual tabletop linens, PlumpJack Wines for an array of California bottlings, and Marina Super, a small neighborhood market with an Italian soul. Lucca, an old-time Italian delicatessen on Chestnut, makes hearty sandwiches and superb fresh ravioli.

The Richmond

Often referred to as San Francisco's New Chinatown, the Richmond is more accurately pan-Asian. Thai, Burmese, Cambodian, and Korean restaurants provide plenty of options for budget diners, while the New May Wah Supermarket and the small housewares shops on Clement Street supply every Asian kitchen need from Thai fish sauce to electric rice cookers. The neighborhood has also long been the commercial heart of the city's small Russian community, harboring Russian tearooms, bakeries, and delicatessens.

The Sunset

A residential district that is home to a rich ethnic mix, the Sunset has no pretensions to trendiness or fashion. Restaurants are modestly priced; shops and markets have what real people need. The locals love Park Chow for Italian food, San Tung for Chinese noodles, Beanery for fresh-roasted coffee, and Polly Ann for exotic ice creams.

The Financial District and Union Square

Numerous coffee bars and sandwich shops cater to downtown office workers with limited lunch time, some of whom grab a slice of pizza on the street at Blondie's or a grilled Italian *panino* (sandwich) at Palio Paninoteca. Expense-account lunchers head for Farallon, Campton Place, Postrio, or the tucked-away Anjou. Clustered around Belden Place is San Francisco's French Quarter, with Café Claude, Café Bastille, and Plouf all but transporting diners to Paris. The venerable Le Central, complete with zinc bar, is nearby, too.

SoMa

Long a gritty area of the city, with auto garages and light manufacturing, SoMa (South of Market) underwent a renaissance in the 1980s and was the hub of the 1990s technology boom. Many of the tech firms are gone, but design, photography, and graphic arts firms remain, and stylish restaurants have sprung

up to serve them. Among the most popular restaurants are Bizou, Bacar, Fringale, Lulu, and Hawthorne Lane.

Pacific Heights and Japantown

Many of the city's well-heeled residents live in Pacific Heights, luring upscale merchants to serve them. Bryan's Quality Meats in Laurel Village is the city's carriage-trade fish and meat purveyor. The petite Artisan Cheese on California Street doesn't have a lot of cheese, just the best. The nearby French bakery Bay Bread provides baguettes and galettes for the neighborhood. Around the corner, the popular Chez Nous, which shares ownership with Bay Bread, offers small plates with a Mediterranean theme.

Japantown draws locals seeking a restorative bowl of hot soba (buckwheat noodles) or ingredients for Japanese recipes. Noodle lovers flock to Mifune in the Japan Center for soba and udon (wheat noodles), while sushi fans might choose Isobune. Soko

Hardware, across from Japan Center, provides sake sets and glazed tea pots and tableware, and the Super Mira grocery supplies all the meat, fish, produce, and packaged goods needed for an authentic Japanese meal.

North Berkeley

Home of the Gourmet Ghetto, a tight-knit community of food merchants with Chez Panisse as the epicenter, North Berkeley draws serious foodies from around the bay. Their destinations: the Cheese Board on Shattuck; Monterey Fish and Monterey Foods on Hopkins; and Acme Bread and Kermit Lynch Wine Merchant on San Pablo Avenue. Two other wine purveyors—North Berkeley Wine on Martin Luther King Jr. Way and Odd Lots in nearby Albany—make this area a good resource for wine fans. Many shoppers begin or end excursions with breakfast or lunch at the delightful Café Fanny.

Rockridge

A walkers' neighborhood with College Avenue as its commercial core, sunny Rockridge brings food lovers to Oakland. They know they can put a whole meal together at the Market Hall, with its collection of small shops specializing in meat, fish, produce, bread, pasta, cheese, and wine. Others come for the top notch restaurants: Oliveto, Citron, À Côté, and Grasshopper. For many in the neighborhood, a latte and a scone at the Oliveto Café is the only way to begin the day.

Marin County

Picturesque Marin County, just across the Golden Gate Bridge from San Francisco, offers a comfortable, semirural home base for many who commute daily into the city. The county's food enthusiasts gather twice weekly at the Marin Civic Center farmers' market, one of the state's finest. The Mill Valley Market and Woodlands Market in Kentfield also provision area homes with high-quality foods, while those who would rather make reservations head for Lark Creek Inn, Insalata's, or the raw-food temple Roxanne's.

Sonoma County

Although wine grapes are the region's main agricultural crop, several small, diversified family farms still thrive in the county. The best place to see their wares is at the Saturday morning Healdsburg farmers' market, a bonanza of locally grown apples, tomatoes, peppers, plums, and flowers. The nationwide housewares merchant Williams-Sonoma got its start in the town of Sonoma in 1956, when Chuck Williams took over a hardware store and stocked it with all the necessities for home cooks interested in French cooking. The county offers superb and varied dining options, among them Zazu in Santa Rosa, popular for its fresh and unfussy Mediterranean menu; Santi in Geyserville, for Italian-inspired fare, and Café La Haye in Sonoma, for contemporary California cooking.

Napa Valley

The world-famous Napa Valley wines drive the economy here, luring tourists and supporting numerous fine restaurants. Locals shop for groceries at the family-run Sunshine Foods or at the St. Helena farmers' market. They pick up cheese at Keller's; pasta, oil, and salami at the Napa Valley Olive Oil Co.; and smoked salmon, caviar, and other delicacies from Dean & DeLuca or the Oakville Grocery. Favorite spots for casual meals include Foothill Café in Napa, for baby back ribs or roast chicken; Napa's Zuzu, a hip spot specializing in small plates; and Mustards in Yountville, long popular for its wine list and casual California style. Diners looking for a more formal experience might head for Terra in St. Helena, where chef Hiro Sone weaves Asian ingredients into his contemporary fare.

GOLDEN GATE BRIDGE

PACIFIC OCEAN

PRESIDIO

LINCOLN PARK

PALACE OF THE LEGION OF HONOR

California St

Clement St

Geary Blvd

S A N

RICHMOND

Balboa St

46th Av

40th Av

33rd Av

26th Av

19th Av

Park Presidio Blvd

9th Av

Fulton St

Cross Over Dr

DE YOUNG MUSEUM

JAPANESE TEA GARDEN

CALIFORNIA ACADEMY OF SCIENCES

GOLDEN GATE PARK

Lincoln Way

SUNSET

46th Av

40th Av

33rd Av

26th Av

19th Av

14th Av

9th Av

The Great Highway

FOREST HILL

Inset map:

Healdsburg

Calistoga

Bodega Bay

Sebastopol

St Helena

Tomales

SONOMA COUNTY

NAPA VALLEY

Inverness

Petaluma

Yountville

Pt Reyes Station

Sonoma

Napa

MARIN

San Rafael

San Francisco

Berkeley

Oakland

PENINSULA

EAST BAY

Half Moon Bay

SOUTH BAY

BAY AREA

N

0   20 mi
0   20 km

Santa Cruz

N

0   .5   1 mi
0   .5   1 km

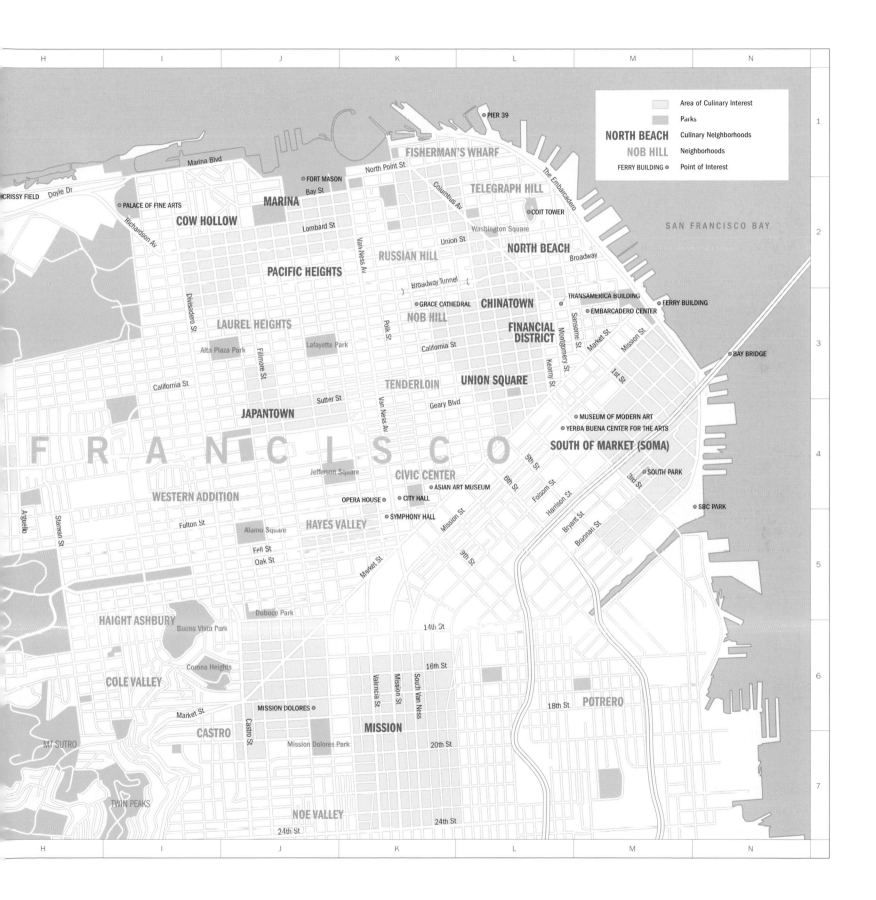

PIER 39

FISHERMAN'S WHARF

Marina Blvd

FORT MASON
North Point St

TELEGRAPH HILL

CRISSY FIELD
Doyle Dr

PALACE OF FINE ARTS

Richardson Av

MARINA

Bay St

Columbus Av

COW HOLLOW

Lombard St

COIT TOWER

Washington Square

SAN FRANCISCO BAY

The Embarcadero

Van Ness Av

RUSSIAN HILL

Union St

NORTH BEACH

Broadway

PACIFIC HEIGHTS

Broadway Tunnel

Divisadero St

LAUREL HEIGHTS

Lafayette Park

GRACE CATHEDRAL

CHINATOWN

NOB HILL

TRANSAMERICA BUILDING

EMBARCADERO CENTER

Sansome St

FERRY BUILDING

Alta Plaza Park

Fillmore St

California St

Polk St

California St

Montgomery St

Market St

Mission St

FINANCIAL
DISTRICT

BAY BRIDGE

California St

Sutter St

TENDERLOIN

UNION SQUARE

Kearny St

1st St

JAPANTOWN

Van Ness Av

Geary Blvd

MUSEUM OF MODERN ART

F R A N C I S C O

YERBA BUENA CENTER FOR THE ARTS

SOUTH OF MARKET (SOMA)

Jefferson Square

CIVIC CENTER

5th St

6th St

SOUTH PARK

3rd St

WESTERN ADDITION

ASIAN ART MUSEUM

OPERA HOUSE
CITY HALL

Folsom St

Fulton St

Alamo Square

HAYES VALLEY

SYMPHONY HALL

Mission St

Harrison St

SBC PARK

Bryant St

Brannan St

Fell St
Oak St

9th St

Market St

Duboce Park

HAIGHT ASHBURY

Buena Vista Park

14th St

Corona Heights

16th St

COLE VALLEY

South Van Ness

18th St

POTRERO

Market St

MISSION DOLORES

Valencia St

Mission St

MT SUTRO

CASTRO

Castro St

Mission Dolores Park

MISSION

20th St

TWIN PEAKS

NOE VALLEY

24th St

24th St

Arguello

Stanyan St

Legend:
Area of Culinary Interest
Parks
NORTH BEACH Culinary Neighborhoods
NOB HILL Neighborhoods
FERRY BUILDING ● Point of Interest

Best of **SAN FRANCISCO**

Bay Area bakeries produce an estimated three and a half million sourdough loaves a week. Some of the original producers, such as Boudin and Parisian, have become big businesses, leaving a niche for small artisan bakers that rely on time-honored methods.

ARTISAN BREAD

Since gold rush days, San Francisco has been synonymous with sourdough bread, a thick-crusted, chewy loaf with a pronounced tang. The ancient practice of leavening bread with a starter—a piece of dough from the previous batch—probably came to California with European immigrants, who brought their starters with them. But in coastal, foggy San Francisco, the starters produced bread with a distinctive sour flavor.

Boudin Bakery, opened by French immigrant Isidore Boudin in 1849, is one of the oldest businesses in San Francisco. The sourdough bread he made famous remains a city trademark. But since the early 1980s, the Bay Area's bread scene has expanded like warm dough. At least a dozen artisan bakeries now cater to customers who care deeply about how their bread tastes.

It is always difficult to pinpoint the birth of a trend, but many would say that the Bay Area's bread revolution began when Steve Sullivan left Chez Panisse to open Berkeley's Acme Bakery in 1983. His sweet baguettes and *pain au levain* (starter-risen bread) quickly became regional standards.

Sullivan's success inspired others to believe that they could earn a living making bread the old-fashioned way. Grace Baking, started in Oakland in 1987 by Glenn Mitchell, is now a sizable wholesale-only business. The company's Pugliese, a dense, flour-dusted loaf, has prompted many imitators. Semifreddi's, another East Bay original, is known for its seeded baguette. La Farine, a small Oakland bakery opened in the 1970s, ramped up its bread output when Acme veteran Jeff Dodge bought it in 1997.

Kathleen Weber never intended to bake for anyone but friends and family, but her wood-oven breads caught the eyes of local chefs. Today, Della Fattoria, her home-based bakery in Petaluma, produces rustic, hand-shaped loaves in two wood-fired ovens for select restaurant and retail accounts.

A number of prominent bakeries began as neighborhood stores whose reputation grew beyond their original address. Noe Valley Bakery, opened in 1995 by newlyweds Michael and Mary Gassen, now sells its fruit breads to many retail markets. Bay Bread began as a charming shop in 1999. Today, owner Pascal Rigo's empire includes four bakeries, all of them renowned for their ultra-French loaves and pastries. Locals flock to Tartine, a petite bakery-café in the Mission, for frangipane croissants and brioche.

What passerby can resist the aroma of just-baked bread and buttery pastry?

Despite the advent of rapid-rise yeast, most professional bakers agree that bread requires a long fermentation to develop flavor and texture. That's the theory behind sourdough bread, which depends on the airborne bacteria and wild yeasts nurtured in a starter, not commercial yeast, for its rise and tang. At Berkeley's Acme Bread, the crusty sourdough *bâtard* is truly slow food.

Sourdough Starter

Steve Sullivan created his first starter for Acme Bread Company with the help of wild yeasts on unsprayed wine grapes, which he steeped in a flour-and-water slurry. Other bakers make their starter with potatoes, rich in the sugar required to feed wild yeasts. All starters need monitoring so they don't become sluggish or too sour. "They can change character daily," says Sullivan. "They reflect their environment." Occasionally a tired starter must be replaced, and some bakers replace them annually.

Ovens

One key element determining bread's character is the oven used to bake it. At Della Fattoria, a small, family-run business in Petaluma, bakers use wood-fired ovens to give their loaves a rustic character. Wood-oven baking involves considerable skill and expense. Instead of setting a thermostat to bring the oven to the desired temperature, as a home baker does, Della Fattoria's bakers must learn how to achieve the temperature they need by manipulating the amount and placement of the wood. Their ovens do contain probes that indicate the temperature in various spots, but such ovens are erratic and uneven, demanding the baker's full attention. When the oven reaches the appropriate temperature, the coals are swept out and the loaves go in.

At Acme Bread Company, the sourdough *bâtard* bakes in stone-hearth deck ovens. Sullivan believes that baking on the heat-retentive stone surface, as opposed to labor-saving racks, gives his loaves a better all-over crust and internal structure.

Making Sourdough Bâtards

BUILDING THE STARTER At Acme, the transformation of a soupy starter into a warm sour *bâtard* is a multistep process that takes about thirty-six hours. First, the starter must be built up gradually with the addition of flour and water in stages.

MIXING AND FERMENTING When the bakers have sufficient starter for the recipe, plus enough to set aside for the next bake, they make a doughlike sponge by adding more flour and water. The sponge ferments for several hours, then is built up into the final dough with the addition of salt, more flour, and water. This dough ferments for several hours to allow the yeasts to multiply and the acid-producing bacteria to do their work.

SHAPING, SLASHING, AND BAKING Next, the dough is divided into portions, left to rest briefly, then shaped into loaves by hand and transferred to flour-dusted cloths for final proofing. Just before baking, the loaves are slashed to allow for even expansion and to create eye-appealing hills and valleys on the surface. Finally, they are moved to stone-hearth ovens to bake for forty minutes.

BAGUETTE

SAN FRANCISCO
SOURDOUGH

CHEESE BOARD
CHEESE ROLLS

BAGUETTE

Modeled after the slender French loaf, the baguette is a staple in Bay Area homes. Several local bakeries produce both sweet and sour versions. Baguettes go stale quickly and need to be eaten within a day, although many cooks slice and toast day-old baguettes for salad croutons or crostini. In the East Bay, La Farine Bakery makes sweet, crusty, rustic baguettes that sell out early on weekends, and Semifreddi's Bakery makes a popular version heavily crusted with sesame, poppy, caraway, and fennel seeds.

CHEESE BOARD CHEESE ROLLS

Customers shopping at the Cheese Board in Berkeley cannot fail to notice when the day's cheese rolls are done. The scent of hot toasted cheese and warm yeasty bread is intoxicating, luring people in from the street. Made from a sourdough whole-wheat (wholemeal) bread dough and two kinds of grated cheese, these rich, savory buns are the ultimate afternoon snack.

SAN FRANCISCO SOURDOUGH

San Francisco's most famous loaf has a thick crust, a chewy texture, and a lively tang thanks to bacteria naturally present in the starter. Named *Lactobacilli sanfrancisco* and abundant in the foggy San Francisco air, these hardworking bacteria produce the lactic acid that makes the bread so delightfully sour. Even when using freeze-dried *L. sanfrancisco,* bakers elsewhere cannot duplicate the taste. Boudin Bakery has the city's oldest starter in continuous use since 1849 when the bakery's founder carried it from Mexico.

MEYER LEMON–ROSEMARY

One of several superb breads made by Della Fattoria, a tiny, family-run Petaluma bakery that utilizes wood-fired ovens, the fragrant Meyer lemon–rosemary loaf is a top seller. Locals find Della Fattoria bread at the Ferry Plaza farmers' market and at some specialty-food stores and upscale markets.

NINE-GRAIN

Wholesome multigrain breads find a large audience in the Bay Area. The mix of grains varies but may include oats, cracked wheat, wheat germ, quinoa, amaranth, cornmeal, millet, and buckwheat.

NINE-GRAIN

FOCACCIA

LEVAIN

MEYER LEMON–
ROSEMARY

PUGLIESE

MORNING BUNS

PUGLIESE

Named for a style of bread made in the southern Italian region of Apulia (Puglia in Italian), Pugliese is a rustic bread made with flour, water, yeast, and salt. Several Bay Area bakeries produce this loaf, or its close cousin the *ciabatta,* although they interpret the style differently. The Pugliese from Artisan Bakers is long, chewy, and light, with multiple air pockets. The version from Grace Baking is also elongated, but the crumb is more dense and uniform.

FOCACCIA

A yeasted flat bread of Italian heritage, focaccia resembles a thick pizza and is usually baked in large slabs. Toppings can be as simple as olive oil and salt but often include a thin layer of thick tomato sauce or slices of fresh tomato and roasted peppers (capsicums), onion, a mixture of herbs, marinated olives, or cheese. San Franciscans rave about the soft, floppy focaccia at Liguria Bakery in North Beach, but other bakeries, such as Semifreddi's in the East Bay, turn out excellent versions as well.

MORNING BUNS

Created by La Farine Bakery on College Avenue in Oakland, morning buns are a neighborhood addiction. When they emerge from the oven, this petite shop fills with the aromas of cinnamon and caramelized sugar. Made with a buttery croissant dough and filled with brown sugar, morning buns are light, flaky, and hard to resist—especially with a steaming cup of strong coffee from the nearby Royal Coffee.

LEVAIN

Made with a starter, *levain* bread modeled on the French *pain au levain* depends on wild yeasts for leavening. In that way, *levain* resembles sourdough, and San Francisco sourdough is a type of *levain.* To trap wild yeasts, a baker mixes a starter of flour and water. Within days, yeasts from the air multiply in the starter, creating the leavening power a bread dough needs. Every batch of *levain* dough includes some starter, which is continually refreshed with more flour and water. In the Bay Area, Acme Bakery's walnut *levain* is a fine example of the genre.

In the 1950s, North Beach's low rents lured artists and writers, who gathered in the neighborhood coffeehouses to read poetry and talk about jazz. Vesuvio Café on Columbus became one of the chief hangouts of this countercultural Beat generation.

COFFEE CENTRAL

On most mornings, the aroma of roasting coffee perfumes North Beach like incense. The neighborhood's coffee roasters—Graffeo, Caffè Malvina, Caffè Roma, and Caffè Trieste—are preparing their daily beans, producing the area's signature scent.

Great coffee has fueled San Francisco since gold rush days, when James Folger launched his coffee-roasting company in the city. By the 1870s, San Francisco's status as a major West Coast port encouraged others to get into the business. Hills Bros. and MJB set up roasting operations in the city—the former in 1878, the latter in 1881—and built family fortunes on the tropical bean.

Roasting beans on the same spot in North Beach since 1935, Graffeo supplies many quality-conscious Bay Area restaurants and homes. The company makes only a light

and a dark roast, but will blend the two to customer taste. Fifty-fifty? Not a problem.

Although North Beach boasts the highest concentration of roasters, other neighborhoods have options for coffee fans. In the Sunset, customers can pick up fresh-roasted beans at Beanery; in the Haight, java fanatics go to Coffee, Tea and Spice.

For some devotees, the only coffee worth drinking is Mr. Espresso, roasted over an oak fire in Oakland, then shipped to retail markets and restaurants. For others, the path to good coffee begins and ends at Peet's. This Berkeley original may be publicly traded now, with stores all over the Bay Area and beyond, but Peet's still defines great coffee for many.

With its European sensibilities, San Francisco has long nurtured a lively café scene and encouraged the fine art of hanging

out. Long before Starbucks arrived, San Franciscans were sipping cappuccinos at Caffè Trieste (opened in 1956) and at Beat hangouts like Vesuvio Café. Thomas Cara, whose delightful shop on Pacific Avenue in the city's Financial District specializes in home espresso machines, claims to have brought the first espresso machine west of the Mississippi shortly after World War II.

Now every San Franciscan has his or her favorite place to nurse a latte. Many still love the North Beach establishments, like the cozy Mario's Bohemian Cigar Store and the bohemian Caffè Trieste. Others feel more at home in small neighborhood spots, like Russian Hill's Le Petit Café or South Park's Caffè Centro. In the evenings, an artsy crowd gathers at Tosca in North Beach, where the house cappuccino is "corrected" with brandy.

A steaming, frothy cappuccino warms a foggy San Francisco afternoon.

ICED COFFEE

CAPPUCCINO

MACCHIATO

ESPRESSO

COFFEE

COFFEE

Whether they are buying coffee in a café or preparing it at home, San Franciscans expect their brew to be dark, rich, and aromatic, from freshly roasted beans. Most Bay Area coffee drinkers purchase whole beans from a local company that roasts them often, such as Peet's or Graffeo, and grind the beans as needed at home. They then typically make their coffee in a drip or plunger-type pot.

ICED COFFEE

Any coffee beverage can be iced to make it more refreshing on a hot day. For the best results, the coffee should be cooled before pouring it over ice to prevent dilution. One of the most delightful iced coffees available in the Bay Area is the version served at Vietnamese restaurants. A blend of condensed milk, strong dark roast coffee, and ice, it is always served in a tall glass with a spoon.

ESPRESSO

Many San Franciscans like to end a restaurant meal with a tiny cup of dense, intense espresso. It is made by forcing hot water through very finely ground, compressed coffee. For the best result, use only high-quality beans for espresso. If properly made, the resulting brew will have more flavor, body, and aroma than filtered coffee and will have a *crema,* or thick, pale, creamy layer on top. Espresso is always strong but should not be overly bitter. It is appropriate to sweeten espresso with sugar, but milk is never added.

CAPPUCCINO

Made with espresso and steamed milk, but with considerably less milk than a latte, a cappuccino has an airy, foamy layer of steamed milk on top. Some like to dust the foam with cocoa powder or cinnamon. A cappuccino is usually served in a coffee cup and makes a satisfying breakfast beverage or afternoon pick-me-up. Coffee connoisseurs believe it is too rich for drinking after dinner.

LATTE

MOCHA

CHAI

HERBAL TEA

GREEN TEA

MACCHIATO

A *macchiato* is an espresso topped with a small spoonful or two of steamed milk. *Macchiato* means "marked" in Italian.

LATTE

Short for the Italian *caffèlatte* (coffee with milk), a latte is made by diluting espresso with a large quantity of hot steamed milk. It is typically served in a tall glass or a ceramic latte bowl. A soothing and satisfying beverage, a latte is most appropriate as a breakfast drink when it is enjoyed with a croissant, muffin, or other morning treat.

MOCHA

Short for *caffè mocha,* a mocha is a chocolate-flavored latte. It may be made with chocolate milk or with chocolate added to milk. It is often topped with whipped cream and a dusting of cocoa powder.

CHAI

Borrowed from the Indian tradition, *chai* is a popular beverage in cafés and specialty-coffee shops. It is a creamy, aromatic, spiced tea made with black tea, sugar or honey, milk, and spices such as ginger, cinnamon, peppercorns, and clove. It appeals any time of day and can be enjoyed hot or iced.

HERBAL TEA

Many Bay Area tea lovers avoid caffeine for health reasons, instead choosing teas made from dried herbs or flowers. Specialty shops and some supermarkets offer a wide selection, such as hibiscus, chamomile, chrysanthemum, and peppermint. They contain no tea leaves, and thus no caffeine. A number of top restaurants, including Chez Panisse, offer an enticing menu of tisanes, or fresh herbal infusions, for sipping after dinner.

GREEN TEA

Green tea leaves come from the same plant as black tea, but the leaves have not been fermented. Their aromas may be grassy, floral, or even smoky. To prevent the tea from tasting bitter, most green teas should be brewed with water that is not boiling—typically, between 160°F (71°C) and 180°F (82°C), depending on the type of tea— and for only two or three minutes. Some people mistakenly believe that green tea has no caffeine. Although it contains less caffeine than coffee or black tea, it is not caffeine free.

When the Mendocino Brewing Company opened in Hopland in 1983, it was only the second brew pub to open since Prohibition. Its success encouraged others, launching a craft-brewing renaissance that shows no sign of slowing.

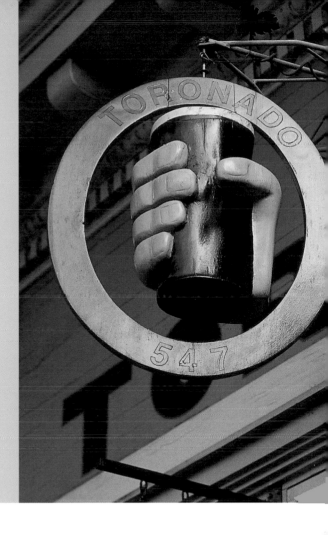

CRAFT BEER

When it comes to beer, San Franciscans are not only discriminating but also provincial. In their affections, nothing surpasses Anchor Steam, the local brew made in a showplace brewery on Potrero Hill. Fritz Maytag, who stepped in to save the brewery in 1965, is a local hero often credited with reviving craft brewing in the United States. Maytag, great-grandson of the washing-machine pioneer, was not looking to buy a brewery when he learned Anchor Steam was about to close. He had never made beer and spent several years upgrading the brewery and mastering brewing techniques. By 1971, he had a product he was willing to bottle and sell.

Maytag kept the beer's peculiar name, whose origins are shrouded in fog and time. Some say that "steam beer" was a nineteenth-century term for West Coast beers made in primitive conditions without ice. In any case, Anchor Brewing Company is no longer primitive; its methods are traditional, but the facility, with its gleaming copper kettles, is state of the art.

Amber and full flavored, with a thick, creamy head, Anchor Steam has inspired numerous other brewers to try their hand at small-production craft beer. The Mendocino Brewing Company's Red Tail Ale has a well-deserved fan club. And Sierra Nevada, originally small, has been so successful with its Pale Ale and other brews that it long ago left microbrewery status behind.

One sign of the Bay Area's healthy interest in full-flavored beer is the sheer number of local brew pubs, which make beer on the premises. San Francisco alone boasts ThirstyBear, Gordon Biersch, Beach Chalet, San Francisco Brewing Company, and Magnolia Brewing Pub. Berkeley has Triple Rock Brewery and Pyramid Brewery, and Oakland is home to Pacific Coast Brewery.

Before Prohibition, most American communities of any size had at least one brew pub. These establishments didn't survive the "dry" years, and it wasn't until the 1980s that a national brew pub revival began, with Northern California leading the way. The Mendocino Brewing Company in Hopland opened in 1983 and is still thriving. Triple Rock opened two years later, and the next decade brought dozens more, all dedicated to brewing craft beer on a small scale.

Beer aficionados know that one of the best places to sample the wares of Northern California's microbreweries is at Toronado, a small bar in San Francisco's Haight District.

LAGER

BOCK

PALE ALE

AMBER ALE

WHEAT BEER

WHEAT BEER

In summer, many microbreweries produce a beer made with some proportion of malted wheat in addition to malted barley. Wheat beer is lighter, crisper, and more refreshing than beer made from barley alone. It is a thirst-quenching brew to enjoy in warm weather with summer foods, such as salads and grilled fish. San Francisco's Anchor Brewing Company makes a wheat beer annually and claims to have revived the style in this country.

LAGER

German brewers developed the methods for lager several centuries ago. *Lager* means "to store" in German, and an authentic lager is fermented at cold temperatures, then stored at even colder temperatures for several weeks or several months. Over that time, the beer develops flavor and becomes naturally carbonated. Although Northern California's artisan breweries produce primarily ales, one exception is Gordon Biersch, a lager specialist. Many lagers are light in body and color but can also be dark, malty, and rich.

PALE ALE

A style that originated in England, pale ale is popular among Northern California brewers and beer drinkers. It is pale only in relation to porters and stouts; most pale ale is golden or amber. Like other ales, pale ales are fermented at relatively warm temperatures and richly hopped, giving them an appealing bitterness and spicy, complex aroma. Sierra Nevada Pale Ale is a prime example of the style and accommodates savory dishes of all kinds.

BOCK

Intended as a spirit-sustaining brew for cold weather, bock is typically a brewery's strongest beer, with alcohol content upward of 6 percent. Full-bodied, malty, and filling, most bocks are lagers that range from golden to dark.

AMBER ALE

A popular style in microbreweries, amber ales tend to have deeper color and richer, maltier flavor than pale ales due to the use of richly roasted malt. Boont Amber from Anderson Valley Brewing and Albion Amber from Marin Brewing are two of the best.

STEAM

PORTER

STOUT

CHRISTMAS ALE

FRUIT BEER

STEAM

The origins of the term *steam beer* are unknown, but the name apparently relates to methods of brewing beer on the West Coast in prerefrigeration days, without ice. Anchor Brewing Company of San Francisco revived the name in the 1970s and trademarked it; today Anchor Steam is this company's signature beer and a modern classic. Amber colored with a creamy texture and long-lasting head, Anchor Steam balances nutty malt aromas with the bracing, bitter character of hops.

PORTER

A rich, dark beer with chocolate, coffee, and caramel notes, porter is a beer to sip and savor slowly. The deep color and intense flavor come from heavily roasting the malted barley. Porters generally have a creamy texture, a thick head, and smooth, malty flavors. They complement beef stews and steak, mushroom dishes, smoked meats, and desserts featuring nuts or chocolate.

STOUT

As the name suggests, stouts are rich, hearty, warming brews that are most inviting in cold weather. Their color is chocolate brown, almost black, and they have big, roasted, chocolate-like aromas, a creamy texture, and a malty flavor. Sierra Nevada Brewing Company and Mendocino Brewing Company are two exceptional Northern California producers of high-quality stout. Pour stout with raw oysters, smoked fish or shellfish, bean soups, and stews. Many stout connoisseurs enjoy it with rich desserts, especially chocolate.

CHRISTMAS ALE

A few Northern California artisan breweries have adopted the tradition of crafting a rich celebration beer at holiday time. The recipe may be the same every year or, as with Anchor Brewing Company's Christmas Ale, each year's brew may be distinctly different.

FRUIT BEER

Some brewers disdain them as frivolous, but fruit beers have a long tradition. Usually made with a malted-wheat base and flavored with raspberry, apricot, or other summer fruits, they are light and thirst-quenching options.

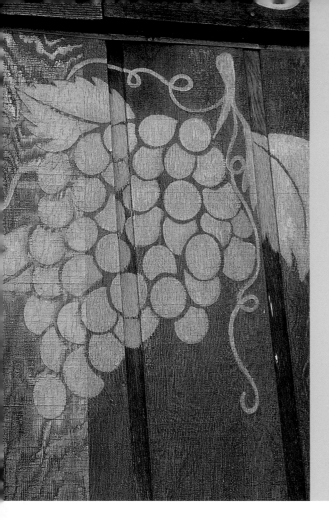

For California vintners, 1976 is a landmark year. That's when French judges at a prominent Paris blind tasting put two California wines—a Napa Valley Cabernet Sauvignon and Chardonnay—in first place, above esteemed French producers.

WINE

Northern California had established a fine reputation for wine as early as the 1880s, with respected wineries in Napa, Sonoma, Santa Clara, and Contra Costa counties. A handful of today's wineries—among them, Gundlach-Bundschu, Charles Krug, Beringer, Chateau Montelena, Simi, and Wente—have their roots in the nineteenth century. But as the fledgling industry began steady growth, two events dealt a near-deadly blow. The first was the arrival and spread of phylloxera, a root-destroying insect. Between 1880 and 1900, it devastated many vineyards. Two decades later, in 1919, the enactment of Prohibition sent Northern California's wine industry into a long slumber.

Not until the 1970s, when a winery revival began in the region, did wines from Napa and Sonoma counties regain and even surpass their earlier acclaim. Thanks in part to the enology and viticulture department at the nearby University of California at Davis, a world leader in research and training, Europeans now come to California to study and intern at local wineries.

Napa Valley produces a wide range of white and red wine varietals, but Cabernet Sauvignon is king. Leading areas for Cabernet production in the valley include Rutherford, Spring Mountain, Howell Mountain, and the Stags Leap District. In the cooler Carneros region (page 133), an area that straddles Napa and Sonoma counties, Chardonnays and Pinot Noirs mature to perfection. Acacia, Etude, and Saintsbury are regional stars.

Rival Sonoma County can claim some of the state's leading Zinfandel and Sauvignon Blanc producers, especially in the Dry Creek Valley area. Alexander Valley Cabernet Sauvignons are somewhat more herbaceous than the berrylike Napa Valley Cabernets, but many collectors seek them out. Jordan Winery and Silver Oak make prized Cabernets from Alexander Valley. The Russian River Valley is Pinot Noir country; Rochioli, Williams Selyem, and Gary Farrell are among the highly regarded Pinot Noir producers here. Sonoma County Chardonnays from Peter Michael, Matanzas Creek, Kistler, and Chateau St. Jean also have a large following.

Bay Area wine merchants offer what may be the best wine shopping anywhere—the local wines, of course, but also bottlings from elsewhere. Top shops include K & L Wine Merchants, the Wine Club, D & M Wine, John Walker, Kermit Lynch Wine Merchant, Marin Wine Cellar, and the Rare Wine Company.

Winemakers exemplify patience, waiting for grapes to ripen and wine to evolve.

Good winemaking is a skillful blend of art and science. The best winemakers combine knowledge of vine physiology and fermentation with a creative vision about how wine should taste. The winemaker's challenge is to use that science to steer vine and wine in the right direction, toward a subjective aesthetic ideal. In fine winemaking, there is no recipe.

Vineyards

Winemakers like to say that good wine isn't made, it's grown. Winemaking begins in the vineyard, with the critical step of planting the right vine in the right place. Each grape varietal has particular soil and climatic needs, so growers take pains to plant appropriately. For many growers, the aim is a "balanced vine," one that stops growing when it has produced just enough leaves, and therefore the ideal conditions, to mature its crop.

Barrel Aging

Oak barrels, at a cost of several hundred dollars each, are an essential ingredient in fine winemaking and among a winery's largest expenses. Red wines aged in small new oak barrels pick up flavor and tannins from the wood, developing more complexity and enhancing their ability to mature gracefully. Tannins give red wines backbone, or structure. Because tannins inhibit oxidation, they also slow the aging process.

France produces most of the barrels used in high-end winemaking, with the wood coming from several different forests. Winemakers spend a lot of time refining their barrel regimen, experimenting with different casks to get the character they want. Some winemakers use a percentage of barrels made from American oak, which imparts a distinctive vanilla-like flavor. Some insist on putting each vintage in new barrels, an expensive proposition. Others use a mix of new and old barrels, possibly as a cost-saving measure, but also, in some cases, because the winemaker believes that using all new oak leaves too great a mark.

Blending Wine

EVALUATING The culmination of a winemaker's annual efforts occurs at blending time, when the winemaking team gathers to evaluate the different lots and create the year's blends.

CHOOSING LOTS Even a winery that bottles one wine will often make several smaller lots of wine, choosing the best or most harmonious for the final blend. The lots may represent different vineyards or parts of the same vineyard. They may represent different techniques; for example, a Chardonnay producer may choose to ferment part of the wine in barrels and part in stainless-steel tanks. And, of course, a winery's lots may represent different grape varieties that complement each other in a blend, such as Cabernet Sauvignon and Merlot.

BLENDING At blending time, the winemaker decides how much of each lot to use to achieve the desired style. Some of California's most prestigious red wines are nonvarietal blends. (Varietal wines must contain at least 75 percent of that varietal.) Instead, the winemaker blends two or more grapes to meet a house style.

SPARKLING WINE

SAUVIGNON BLANC

CHARDONNAY

PINOT NOIR

SYRAH

SPARKLING WINE

In just the last few decades, Northern California's sparkling wines have garnered critical acclaim internationally. Cool regions such as Anderson Valley and Carneros are the premier spots for it. Even so, Northern California's sparkling wines tend to have more fruit and body than French Champagnes, the result of the former's warmer climate.

SAUVIGNON BLANC

Known for its affinity with seafood and salads, crisp Sauvignon Blanc complements Bay Area cooking as well as or better than any other white wine varietal. Some California producers keep it in stainless steel from start to finish to yield a wine in a clean, refreshing style. Others prefer some oak aging to round off the wine's edges and give it more complexity. Grilled fish, seafood, and spring vegetable dishes are good companions for this wine.

CHARDONNAY

California's most famous white wine, Chardonnay tends to display abundant fruit aromas—such as apple, pear, and pineapple—and to have more body than other white wines. Many producers allow Chardonnay to undergo malolactic fermentation to give it a more buttery, rounded character. Oak aging, a common technique, adds a smoky aroma and flavor. Chardonnay is a fine match for pâté, mushrooms, or chicken.

PINOT NOIR

This grape thrives in cool climates, such as the Russian River and Carneros areas. Well-made Pinot Noir often has red-fruit aromas, such as berry, cherry, and plum. The wine tends to be lighter in color, weight, and tannin than Cabernet Sauvignon.

SYRAH

A relative newcomer to Northern California vineyards, Syrah has established itself as a worthy grape. Often characterized as meaty, spicy, or peppery, Syrah is a bold and versatile wine with abundant color, flavor, and aroma.

ZINFANDEL

MERLOT

CABERNET SAUVIGNON

PETITE SIRAH

LATE-HARVEST RIESLING

ZINFANDEL

For years, California claimed Zinfandel as its own, but DNA testing has shown that the grape has a match in Italy's Primitivo. Nevertheless, it is a hometown favorite, with many Bay Area fans. Sonoma's Dry Creek Valley and the Amador County foothills are prime growing areas. Fruity, intense, and moderate in tannins, Zinfandel marries well with many foods, from hamburgers to pasta to steak. Some producers make it in an easy-drinking style; others aim for higher intensity and alcohol.

MERLOT

A red wine that is generally moderate in tannin, Merlot can be enjoyed at a younger age than most Cabernet Sauvignons. Consequently, restaurateurs tend to like it; it doesn't have to be cellared long. California Merlot often has an herbaceous aroma and tends to complement lamb dishes, grilled chicken, and vegetarian main courses.

CABERNET SAUVIGNON

The king of California's red wine grapes, Cabernet Sauvignon is the varietal that most rewards aging. Nevertheless, some of the state's best Cabernet areas, such as the Stags Leap District of Napa Valley, yield wines that are moderate in tannin and delightful when young. Cabernet Sauvignon aromas range from blackberry and plum to coffee and chocolate. The color is typically deep, the flavor intense, and the tannin pronounced. Cabernet Sauvignon is ideal with red meat, whether lamb, beef, or wild game.

PETITE SIRAH

Petite Sirah has had a tangled history in California, with growers attaching the name to different grapes. Only now are researchers beginning to decode its parentage. Valued as a blending wine because of its color and tannin, it is bottled separately by a few vintners who admire its rusticity.

LATE-HARVEST RIESLING

Late-harvest Rieslings make rich, exquisite dessert wines that are compatible with seasonal fruits, such as apricots and cherries. Navarro and Chateau St. Jean are top producers of this wine.

Originating in the teahouses of China's Guangdong province, the first dim sum were probably simple snacks intended to lure patrons. Today, dim sum preparation is a high art, with some of the finest practitioners at San Francisco-area teahouses.

DIM SUM

For many San Franciscans, weekend brunch does not mean eggs Benedict or waffles. Instead, it's the perfect time to go out for dim sum and revel in the clamor and commotion of a Cantonese teahouse at midday.

By late morning on Saturdays and Sundays, the Bay Area's popular dim sum restaurants are packed with multigenerational Chinese families. They have gathered to share a meal of flaky pastries, steamed dumplings, and stuffed buns, all served on small plates and intended to "delight the heart"—a loose translation of dim sum.

In Cantonese, the dim sum meal is known as *yumcha,* literally "drink tea." Traditionally, it is the only Chinese repast accompanied with tea (*cha* is generally served after the food). Large dim sum houses usually offer a selection of teas, from the light and fragrant

chrysanthemum to the robust *pu-erh,* the latter believed to counteract the richness of dim sum.

Modest dim sum establishments may have an à la carte menu or a few servers circulating with trays laden with small plates. But at the larger establishments, which rival any in Hong Kong, food emerges from the kitchen on a steady stream of carts that waiters maneuver through the crowded dining room. As they stroll past, they sing out the names of their dishes—*ha gau* (steamed shrimp dumplings), *siu mai* (open-faced pork and shrimp dumplings), *cha siu bao* (barbecued pork buns)—and diners select the ones they want. You can always beckon a waiter over to get a closer look, and he or she will lift the lids of the bamboo steamer baskets.

At the biggest dim sum houses, the weekend repertoire may include seventy-five

to one hundred choices, from the familiar steamed dumplings and wonton soup to stuffed vegetables, fried squid, barbecued meats, steamed chicken feet, green (spring) onion pancakes, and sweet bean pastries. It is tempting to fill your table with the first tantalizing delights you see, but dim sum enthusiasts know that it pays to be patient.

When you make a selection, the waiter will mark your bill accordingly. Most dishes are moderately priced, but some specialties, such as roast suckling pig, are more costly.

You can experience dim sum at its most bountiful, authentic, and enjoyable at such established restaurants as Gold Mountain, Harbor Village, Ton Kiang, and Yank Sing in San Francisco; Restaurant Peony in Oakland; Hong Kong Flower Lounge in Millbrae; and Koi Palace in Daly City.

Every dim sum parlor has its own repertoire of dishes, but you can count on finding a variety of steamed dumplings; spring rolls; fried dumplings similar to potstickers; barbecued and roasted meats, such as suckling pig and duck; fried squid and fried shrimp (prawns); and a collection of flaky pastries, such as egg custard tarts, and bean-paste sweets.

Dim Sum Vegetables

With its emphasis on dumplings, buns, taro puddings, noodles, and sticky rice, a dim sum meal is carbohydrate heaven. To leaven the feast, diners often choose lighter fare, such as steamed Chinese broccoli (gai lan) with oyster sauce; seaweed salad; or shrimp-stuffed green peppers. If you don't see a steamed or stir-fried vegetable on any of the carts, check the menu on the table or ask a waiter. Most will make greens on request.

Tea

Hot tea served from a teapot in small china cups is as fundamental to dim sum as the dumplings and pastries. Some people refer to dim sum as "Chinese tea lunch" because, historically, the ritual of tea drinking provided the excuse to serve food. Tea, especially black tea, is said to counteract the richness of dim sum. As soon as you are seated, a waiter will appear to take your tea order. (More modest establishments may offer no choice, and a waiter will simply bring the house tea immediately.) There is rarely a tea menu; clients are expected to know what they want.

One of the most popular dim sum teas is *pu-erh,* an unusual tea from China's Yunnan province with a dark color and an earthy or woodsy flavor. *Pu-erh* is fermented, which purportedly enhances its contribution to health. Other diners prefer lighter teas, such as fragrant jasmine (a green or oolong tea scented with jasmine flowers) or caffeine-free chrysanthemum tea.

Making Barbecued Pork Buns

ROLLING DOUGH Cantonese *cha siu bao* (barbe-cued pork buns), served at every dim sum house, begin with sweetened, yeasted wheat-flour dough swiftly flattened into small circles with a rolling pin.

STUFFING AND FORMING The filling includes finely chopped barbecued pork stir-fried with garlic, soy sauce, oyster sauce, and sugar. After the filling cools, chefs use chopsticks to place a small portion in each round. Using fingers, they seal the buns with rapid-fire pinching and pleating.

STEAMING The buns, with their surface swirls, are set aside to rise before steaming. In a hot kitchen, that doesn't take long. Before steaming, each bun is placed on a square of thin paper so it won't stick. Diners must peel the paper off the bun.

SERVING Snow-white *cha siu bao* go from the steamers to the rolling dim sum carts, still in their lidded bamboo baskets. The servers will keep the lids on to keep the buns warm, announcing the contents as they stroll past each table.

CONGEE

CHA SIU BAO

LOTUS-LEAF RICE

STUFFED BELL PEPPERS

CONGEE

Also known as *jook, congee* is Chinese comfort food, eaten for breakfast, late at night, and for dim sum. Made with rice cooked for a long time in broth or water, *congee* resembles a thin soup or porridge. The Chinese genius for contrasting texture and flavor can be seen in the garnishing. Typically, *congee* is topped with a choice of condiments, such as fresh ginger, sesame oil, green (spring) onions, cilantro (fresh coriander), chopped peanuts, or Sichuan preserved vegetable (the stem of a type of mustard green, preserved with chiles and salt).

CHA SIU BAO

The tender, snow white steamed buns known as *cha siu bao* hide a surprise inside: finely chopped and seasoned barbecued pork (see how they are made on page 57). The buns are soft, spongy, and sweet, leavened with yeast and baking powder; the filling is salty, sugary, and intense. The contrast makes *cha siu bao* irresistible. Made by a master dim sum chef, the buns will have neatly pleated tops that make them almost too pretty to eat.

STUFFED BELL PEPPERS

Another popular dim sum offering features small squares of green bell pepper (capsicums) stuffed with a savory, springy filling of ground pork, water chestnuts, dried mushrooms, and sometimes shrimp (prawns). The stuffed peppers are browned first on the filling side, then turned over and steamed until tender. They are eaten with black bean sauce, which the dim sum waiter spoons over them tableside. A similar dim sum calls for using the same filling for stuffed tofu triangles, which are panfried rather than steamed.

LOTUS-LEAF RICE

Neatly wrapped lotus-leaf packages, common on dim sum carts, are snipped open with scissors tableside to reveal their steaming filling: sticky, or glutinous, rice studded with bits of sweet Chinese sausage, dried mushrooms, gingko nuts, cubed chicken, and other savory nuggets. The leaves impart a delicate herbal flavor to the rice but are not eaten.

GREEN ONION PANCAKES

CHICKEN FEET

HA GAU

CUSTARD TARTS

HA GAU

Few customers pass up an order of *ha gau,* or steamed shrimp dumplings. The dumplings' flavor and delicacy, or lack thereof, are an indication of the dim sum chef's skills. Well-made *ha gau* are small, beautifully pleated, and dainty, with thin, translucent wrappers that reveal the filling within. The shrimp stuffing should be well seasoned and balanced. *Ha gau* are usually prepared in small stainless-steel steamers, which are transferred to the diner's table from the cart. They are delicious dipped into a mixture of soy sauce and sesame oil.

GREEN ONION PANCAKES

These hot, crisp cakes begin with soft wheat-flour dough that is rolled into a circle, brushed with lard or oil, sprinkled with minced green (spring) onion and salt, and then rolled up like a jelly roll. Finally, the stuffed roll is coiled like a snake, flattened again with a rolling pin, and panfried until golden and crusty. Ideally, the flaky, fragrant cakes are cut into wedges and served piping hot. In most dim sum houses, green onion pancakes do not circulate on the carts because they must be made to order; you can inquire about their availability from a server.

CHICKEN FEET

Perhaps off-putting to Westerners accustomed to buying chicken without the feet attached, chicken feet are a dim sum delicacy. Steamed and served hot, often with just their juices, they are accompanied by a soy-based dipping sauce. In other dim sum establishments, they may be braised in soy sauce with rock sugar, ginger, and star anise, which turns them golden brown and infuses them with flavor. Dim sum regulars can eat chicken feet gracefully with chopsticks, leaving only tiny cleaned bones behind.

CUSTARD TARTS

One of several sweet options on traditional dim sum carts, custard tarts are among the prettiest. Their lemon yellow filling is rich with eggs and scented with vanilla, and the delicate pastry dissolves on the tongue. Other sweet selections include small pastries filled with sweetened red bean paste, plain steamed cake, and puddings made with water chestnut flour. Deep-fried sesame balls also have many fans. Made with a sweet rice-flour dough wrapped around a nugget of sweet bean paste, then coated with sesame seeds and fried, they are rich and satisfying.

The Bay Area's Asian population is far more diverse than in gold rush days. The early Chinese immigrants have been joined in modern times by Koreans, Japanese, Filipinos, Vietnamese, and others, creating a hungry market for Asian produce.

ASIAN PRODUCE

Not long ago, a San Francisco shopper seeking bok choy or lemongrass would have to head for Chinatown or one of the Asian produce markets on Clement Street. Today, such items are commonplace in Bay Area supermarkets, and the selection of Asian produce in non-Asian markets is growing.

Part of the reason is the city's large Asian population. Over 30 percent of San Francisco County's residents are Asian, and they don't all shop in Chinatown. But the city's non-Asian shoppers are also increasingly reaching for long beans, Asian eggplant (aubergine), Chinese broccoli, and fresh soybeans—foods that many came to know in local restaurants.

Even restaurants with no particular ethnic bent have embraced Asian herbs and vegetables and helped introduce them to a broader audience. At Farallon, one of San

Francisco's premier seafood houses, Monterey prawns might be served with a lemongrass rice cake and pickled shiitake mushrooms. The elegant Masa's in San Francisco pairs Japanese eel with wood ear mushrooms and daikon. And at Terra in St. Helena, where the chef is Japanese but the food is mostly Mediterranean, tender black cod and shrimp dumplings float in *shiso* broth. These influences have given non-Asian home cooks a greater comfort level with Asian produce.

The growing presence of Asian produce in Bay Area markets can also be attributed in part to the work of Hmong farmers in the state's San Joaquin Valley. Today, there are about sixty thousand Hmong in the valley, the largest concentration outside Asia, and they have learned American farming methods with the help of the University of California.

Hmong farmers grow strawberries and cherry tomatoes as well as dozens of varieties of Asian vegetables, such as bitter melon, lemongrass, and daikon.

Although non-Asian supermarkets sell some Asian vegetables, shoppers can find the best selection at Asian markets and farmers' markets in communities with a large Asian population. The farmers' markets in Oakland, Vallejo, and El Cerrito and the Alemany Farmers' Market in San Francisco are excellent sources. So are the many Asian groceries in San Francisco's Richmond and Sunset neighborhoods, such as New May Wah and Sunset Super. The Super Mira market in San Francisco's Japantown satisfies cooks looking for Japanese produce such as burdock, fresh soybeans, and *shiso*. Oakland's vibrant Chinatown is another excellent resource.

ASIAN HERBS

BOK CHOY

LONG BEANS

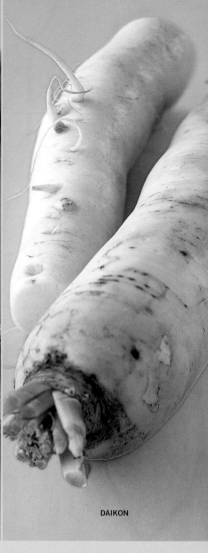

DAIKON

ASIAN HERBS

Bay Area supermarkets generally stock Thai basil and cilantro (fresh coriander), but for the best selection of Asian herbs, shoppers go to local Asian markets. There, they can find a broad selection of the fresh herbs called for in Asian recipes. Among the favorites are kaffir lime leaf, kari leaf, *shiso,* and *rau ram.* Kaffir lime leaves have a citrus fragrance that enlivens Thai soups. Kari leaf, or curry leaf, adds aroma to south Indian dishes. Japanese *shiso,* or perilla, has a minty taste, and *rau ram,* eaten raw, adds its grassy taste to Vietnamese salads.

BOK CHOY

The most typical bok choy has snowy white stems, a noticeably bulbous base, and deep green leaves. It is cut up and added to stir-fries, chow mein, wonton soup, and other dishes in which its mildly bitter flavor is appreciated. Shanghai bok choy, a petite member of the family, has pale green, cupped stems and slightly darker green leaves. It is a great Bay Area favorite, even in non-Asian kitchens, for its shapeliness and mild flavor. Cooks halve it and steam it or add it to soups.

LONG BEANS

The long, skinny green beans known as long beans, yard-long beans, or asparagus beans are unrelated to the green beans familiar to most Western cooks. Long beans are a cousin of black-eyed peas, although the former are always eaten in the pod, not shelled. They have a more intense taste and chewier texture than Blue Lake beans or haricots verts and are often stir-fried, with or without blanching first. They perform best in warm climates, where it is said that you can practically see them grow. Look for beans with few blemishes or wrinkles.

DAIKON

A long, white, relatively mild type of radish, daikon is available in Bay Area supermarkets. The name is Japanese, but daikon is also used in other Asian kitchens, especially Korean. Daikon may be simmered in soups and stews, or pickled, as for kimchi. Bay Area chefs who mix East and West often use it in salads.

ASIAN EGGPLANT

LEMONGRASS

SOYBEANS

BITTER MELON

ASIAN EGGPLANT

Asian markets carry eggplants (aubergines) of remarkable variety. Some are elongated and much more slender than the Western globe eggplant. Others are small, white, and round and about the size of an egg, providing a clue to the source of the vegetable's name. Some Asian eggplants are pale green or streaked with green and white. Others range from pale lavender to purple to almost black. The elongated ones may be used interchangeably in recipes.

LEMONGRASS

An essential seasoning in the Bay Area's Southeast Asian restaurants and an increasingly popular aromatic among non-Asian chefs, lemongrass lends a sprightly citrus flavor to soups, sauces, and braised dishes. Resembling a long, woody green (spring) onion, it must be trimmed of its coarse leafy tops and tough exterior, then very thinly sliced or smashed to release its aroma. Bay Area cooks use it to flavor everything from scallops to sorbet.

SOYBEANS

Known as *edamame* in Japanese, soybeans in the pod have become enormously popular in Bay Area kitchens. Even supermarkets sell them now in the freezer or refrigerated case, precooked and packaged. In summer, you can sometimes find them fresh at farmers' markets or in specialty-produce stores. Fresh soybeans resemble sugar snap peas, although soybean pods are soft and fuzzy and the beans inside are pronounced. Japanese restaurants boil the whole beans in salted water and serve them as a snack.

BITTER MELON

The name speaks the truth. Bitter melon, which looks like a ridged, warty cucumber, is indeed bitter, due to the presence of quinine. For Westerners, it is an acquired taste, but Chinese diners appreciate its cooling nature. The melon is usually seeded with the surrounding seed membrane removed, but not peeled. Typically, it is cooked with pungent ingredients such as chiles and salted black beans.

Spanish missionaries brought the first cattle to California in 1769, thus launching the state's dairy industry. A century later, the state claimed one hundred thousand milk cows, many in the San Francisco area, and commercial cheese making began.

ARTISAN CHEESE

A century ago, Marin County was the state's premier dairy county. Situated just north of San Francisco, the then-rural region enjoyed plentiful spring grass, cool coastal summers, and numerous urban customers. Marin French Cheese Company, established in 1865, is one reminder of those days.

But the picture changed as refrigerated transportation improved. By midcentury, huge Central Valley dairies could deliver milk to San Francisco more cheaply than small Marin and Sonoma dairies could. Many local dairy farmers sold their land to developers, and cheese making in the Bay Area all but ended.

Enter Laura Chenel. In the late 1970s, hoping to generate revenue from her growing herd of Sonoma County goats, Chenel went to France to learn how to make cheese. When she returned, she began to sell her fresh chèvres (goat cheeses) to local restaurants, who eagerly bought them (page 101).

Chenel's success encouraged others, and the Bay Area is now home to about a dozen artisan cheese makers. Unlike the faceless California dairies making commodity cheese, each one of these Bay Area ventures comes with a story. At the tiny Andante Dairy in Santa Rosa, Korean-born cheese maker and musician Soyoung Scanlan gives all her goat's and cow's milk cheeses musical names. Cindy Callahan, a former lawyer, backed into the business of cheese making after she bought some sheep to keep the pasture grasses short on her country property. Now Bellwether Farms, her dairy, is a critically acclaimed producer of sheep's and cow's milk cheeses, among them Carmody, Crescenza, and San Andreas.

In Point Reyes on the Marin coast, cheese maker Sue Conley produces delicious cottage cheese and the luscious triple-cream, washed-rind Red Hawk at the Cowgirl Creamery. At the Joe Matos Cheese Factory, Joe and Mary Matos make an aged Portuguese-style cow's milk cheese called St. George with milk from their herd.

No overview of Bay Area cheese making could fail to mention Ig Vella, whose Vella Cheese Company in Sonoma makes a unique dry jack, an aged cow's milk cheese with a cocoa-dusted rind.

Shoppers can find these local cheeses and a large international selection at the Bay Area's best cheese counters. Aficionados shop at San Francisco's Artisan Cheese, Berkeley's Cheese Board, Pasta Shops in the East Bay, and St. Helena's Dean & DeLuca.

Whether local or shipped from afar, fine cheese is a Bay Area obsession.

Cheese in all its variety is simply milk transformed for long keeping. Farmers long ago learned that coagulating milk and draining the whey yielded a dairy product that could last from weeks to years. Today, Northern California cheese makers use age-old methods to produce pungent blues, aromatic washed-rind cheeses, luscious triple-creams, and more.

Milk

Fresh, high-quality milk is the starting point for artisan cheese making. For that reason, some cheese makers use milk only from their own herds, producing what are known as farmstead cheeses. Others purchase milk from nearby farms. Most use cow's or goat's milk. Sheep's milk makes excellent cheese, but sheep are shy producers, which means limited production and higher prices. In Sonoma County, Bellwether Farms is one of the area's few producers of sheep's milk cheeses.

Aging Cheese

Making a hard cheese capable of long aging requires techniques different from those used for fresh cheese. Cheeses intended to age, such as Vella dry jack, need to have moisture removed because high moisture limits lifespan. If an aged cheese is the goal, a cheese maker will take steps to encourage the fresh curds to expel more whey.

Chief among those possible steps are cutting, cooking, and pressing the curds. Almost all curds are cut before molding, but the size of the cut makes a difference.

Large curds retain more whey, so for an aged cheese, curds are cut small. Heating the curds also causes them to throw off liquid. Finally, once the curds are molded, they can be pressed to draw off even more whey.

Cheese makers can also lengthen a cheese's potential life by encouraging a rind to form. The rind protects the cheese from unwelcome molds while allowing it to release moisture and mature slowly. Rubbing the wheel with salt, brine, or vegetable or olive oil (as for Vella dry jack) helps a rind to form.

Making Mt. Tam Cheese

STARTER At the Cowgirl Creamery in Point Reyes, a batch of Mt. Tam cheese begins with creating a starter culture of bacteria and milk. Overnight, the bacteria feed on the milk sugar, or lactose, and produce lactic acid, causing the milk to curdle. In the morning, this active starter is added to local organic cow's milk to produce lactic acid.

MOLDING Once the bacteria establish themselves in the vat, rennet is added and curds form. Using a wire tool, workers cut the curds and stir them to expel whey, then the curds are drained, washed, and scooped into molds. The cheeses are pressed to extract more whey, then left overnight. The next morning, they're unmolded by hand.

BRINING, DRYING, AND AGING The cheeses float in a brine bath for a couple of hours to season them, and then they air-dry for a day. Finally, they move to the aging room, so that the enzymes and molds can do their transformational work. Over the next two to four weeks, the cheese develops a bloomy white rind; a softer, creamier texture; and a complex range of flavors.

REDWOOD HILL FARM CHEVRE

LAURA CHENEL TAUPINIÈRE

CYPRESS GROVE HUMBOLDT FOG

PELUSO TELEME

BELLWETHER FARMS RICOTTA

COWGIRL CREAMERY RED HAWK

PELUSO TELEME

Giovanni Peluso began making Teleme in the 1930s in Los Banos to satisfy the Italian American demand for a soft, fresh, cow's milk cheese similar to Stracchino. His son and grandson continue the business. Made in a square shape and dusted with rice flour, Teleme has a tangy, yeasty crème fraîche flavor when released at about a month old. If matured for another two to four weeks, it becomes oozy, even runny, and develops mushroomlike flavors.

BELLWETHER FARMS RICOTTA

This small Sonoma County dairy makes two kinds of ricotta: a sheep's milk version using milk from its own herd, and a cow's milk ricotta using Jersey milk from nearby farms. Both begin with whey drained from Bellwether Farms' aged cheeses. Milk is added to the whey and heated, then coagulated with vinegar. The soft, fresh curds are scooped from the vat into small draining baskets, drained overnight, and sold immediately.

REDWOOD HILL FARM CHEVRE

This fresh, fluffy, mild goat cheese is one of several goat cheeses produced by this Sonoma County farm using milk from its own herd. Many Bay Area chefs use it in dishes requiring fresh goat cheese.

LAURA CHENEL TAUPINIÈRE

A soft-ripened goat cheese with a bloomy white rind, Laura Chenel Taupinière can be enjoyed at any stage from two weeks, when it leaves the Sonoma County dairy, to two months. As it matures, it becomes drier inside, creamier under the rind, and much more complex in flavor.

COWGIRL CREAMERY RED HAWK

Produced by Cowgirl Creamery in Point Reyes, Red Hawk is one of America's few artisan washed-rind cheeses. Cheese maker Sue Conley uses cream-enriched organic cow's milk from a nearby dairy. During the six-week aging period, the cheeses are repeatedly washed with brine to encourage flavor-enhancing and moisture-loving surface molds. A ripe Red Hawk has a golden orange rind; a creamy, butter-colored interior; and flavors of earth and spice.

POINT REYES
ORIGINAL BLUE

FISCALINI BANDAGE-
WRAPPED CHEDDAR

MATOS ST. GEORGE

VELLA DRY JACK

CYPRESS GROVE HUMBOLDT FOG

Mary Keehn established Cypress Grove in Humboldt County, in far Northern California, in 1984, with the aim of making goat cheese. She makes several cheeses now, but the star is Humboldt Fog, a wheel with a coating and central layer of ash. As it ages, the cheese develops a soft, white rind and matures from the outside in. A ripe Humboldt Fog is creamy under the rind but firm in the center and is delightful with walnut bread.

POINT REYES ORIGINAL BLUE

The Giacomini family, longtime dairy farmers in Marin County, began making cheese in 2000. Their sole product, Original Blue, made with raw milk from their own herd and aged at least six months, is California's only artisan blue. The result is creamy and tangy.

MATOS ST. GEORGE

Since the 1970s, the Matos family has made an aged cow's milk cheese patterned after a cheese from their homeland, the Azores. Using milk from their own cows, it ages three months before release. The flavor is medium sharp.

FISCALINI BANDAGE-WRAPPED CHEDDAR

John Fiscalini, a third-generation California dairyman from Modesto, moved into cheese making in 2001. With cheese maker Mariano Gonzalez, Fiscalini now produces a magnificent Cheddar in the English style, using his own raw cow's milk. The young sixty-pound (27-kg) wheels are wrapped in cheesecloth—the "bandage"—to allow them to breathe as they mature. An eighteen-month-old wheel has a lingering, nutty flavor and a classic Cheddar texture.

VELLA DRY JACK

An aged cow's milk cheese from Sonoma's Vella Cheese Company, dry jack has won numerous awards. The cheese has a firm, golden interior and a hard rind dusted with cocoa. The regular dry jack is aged seven to ten months; the Special Select is aged longer, producing a cheese with more intense and longer-lasting flavor. Serve the jack with olives before dinner or with nuts or dried fruit at the end of a meal.

The prominent Ghirardelli sign, with its fifteen-foot-high letters, was first illuminated in 1923. Darkened during the war years for defense reasons, it has shined brightly ever since, symbol of America's longest continuously operating chocolate manufacturer.

CHOCOLATE

In 1849, Italian-born Domenico Ghirardelli came to California to pan for gold but stayed to launch a chocolate empire. Today, Ghirardelli Square, company headquarters from the 1890s to the 1960s, is a registered landmark, drawing millions of tourists each year. Ghirardelli Chocolate is presently owned by a Swiss firm, and the products are made in a San Francisco suburb. Nevertheless, the company's highly visible presence cemented the city's reputation for quality chocolate.

The Guittard family added to that image, establishing a chocolate-making operation in San Francisco in 1868. Nowadays, the great-grandson of French-born founder Etienne Guittard runs the company. Building on the growing interest in fine chocolate, Guittard introduced a line of premium chocolate under the E. Guittard label, named for the company

founder. E. Guittard bars are higher in cacao solids, producing the richer bittersweet flavor that top-tier pastry chefs demand. What's more, the company is pioneering single-varietal chocolates, made with only one type of cacao bean, sometimes from a single source. (Most chocolates are blends.)

San Francisco's chocolate story added a new chapter in 1997, when two partners opened Scharffen Berger. Robert Steinberg, a former physician, and John Scharffenberger, a former winery owner, had never made chocolate commercially when they launched their business, but they wanted to make small-batch chocolate from beans they blended and roasted themselves. Today, the company supplies chefs around the country with critically acclaimed semisweet (plain), bittersweet, and unsweetened chocolate.

Several high-end confectioners have also contributed to the Bay Area's renowned chocolate habit. Alice Medrich, a respected cooking teacher, launched the nationwide chocolate truffle craze at her now-shuttered Cocolat stores. Joseph Schmidt, a European-trained baker, opened his Castro-area shop in 1983. His chocolates were an immediate hit, especially the egg-shaped, flavored truffles that became the company's signature. Today, his confections are sold all over the country, but the original Castro store remains. Michael Recchiuti's business was originally wholesale, but in 2003, he opened a boutique in San Francisco's Ferry Building. There, customers can purchase the elegant boxed chocolates that made his gilt-edged reputation. These petite works of art include flavors such as lavender and jasmine.

From bittersweet bars to truffles, chocolate is San Francisco's favorite flavor.

A chocolate bar that snaps cleanly, melts smoothly in the mouth, and delivers a range of enticing flavors is the product of a painstaking manufacturing process. The world's best chocolate producers—among them, Scharffen Berger, Ghirardelli, and Guittard in the San Francisco Bay Area—purchase their beans carefully and handle them with skill.

Cacao

Cacao trees, the source of chocolate, thrive in equatorial climates. Brazil, the Ivory Coast, and Indonesia are large producers, but some of the finest beans come from Ecuador, Trinidad, and Venezuela. Botanists have identified three main cacao strains: criollo, the finest and rarest, yielding exceptional chocolate; forastero, a disease-resistant strain that produces a less desirable chocolate; and trinitario, a hardy hybrid.

Cacao Percentages

In order to appeal to the increasingly sophisticated chocolate consumer, top manufacturers today label their chocolates with the percentage of cacao content by weight. A chocolate bar labeled "64 percent cacao" is 36 percent something else. What else? The largest other component is sugar, but it also contains a hint of vanilla for flavor, a small amount of lecithin for texture, and, in the case of milk chocolate, powdered milk. But because cacao is the source of the chocolate flavor, connoisseurs seeking an intense chocolate experience should look for a bar with a high cacao content. The higher the cacao percentage, the lower the sugar, and the less sweet the chocolate will be. Unsweetened chocolate is 100 percent cacao.

These percentages are a better guide to flavor than terms such as "bittersweet" and "semisweet." American chocolates can be labeled bittersweet with only 35 percent cacao content. Nevertheless, high cacao content is not a guarantee of quality. The beans and the processing are equally, if not more, important.

Making Chocolate

REMOVING THE PULP Transforming beans into bars is a time-consuming process. First, beans are fermented for several days with their pulp, which liquefies and drains away. Then the beans are dried, either mechanically or in the sun.

ROASTING AND CRUSHING At a chocolate factory, the beans are cleaned to remove debris. Then they are roasted in rotating drums, a process that requires the oversight of an experienced roaster. Next, the beans are cracked mechanically and the inedible hulls are winnowed from the nibs, the edible part of the bean. Finally, the nibs are crushed into a paste called cocoa liquor.

MIXING AND FINISHING According to the recipe, sugar, vanilla, and lecithin are added at this point, and the mixture is then conched, or kneaded, for hours to achieve the desired texture and flavor. Tempering to improve appearance and texture, molding the chocolate, and packaging are the final steps in this long journey.

APPETIZERS

San Francisco's favorite appetizers reflect its multiethnic face. Bruschetta,

quesadillas, and Chinese dumplings vie daily for diners' attention.

San Franciscans roam the globe in their passion for appetizers, gathering ideas from the many cultures represented in this international city. From Mexican quesadillas to Chinese dim sum to Italian *bruschetta,* everything is fair game for open-minded San Francisco diners, who love starting meals with an assortment of small plates. It's not uncommon in many Bay Area restaurants for customers to put together a feast of appetizers alone, so popular are the small, savory dishes that typically open a meal. When entertaining at home, many San Franciscans serve the first glass of wine with store-bought olives they have marinated themselves.

OYSTERS ON THE HALF SHELL WITH TWO SALSAS

Oyster fans everywhere enjoy the bivalves with a tangy or tart condiment: a squeeze of lemon or splash of mignonette in France, a spicy cocktail sauce or touch of Tabasco in New Orleans. The farmed Pacific Coast oysters likewise benefit from a pick-me-up that enlivens them without masking their briny flavor. Salsa cruda, using fresh tomatoes, and salsa verde, made with fresh tomatillos, are indispensable sauces in the Mexican kitchen. But pairing these sauces with oysters is a California concept, a variation on the Mexican seafood coctel (cocktail).

1 To make the *salsa cruda,* in a bowl, combine the tomatoes, onion, chile, cilantro, and lime juice. Stir to mix, then season to taste with salt. Let stand for 15 minutes to blend the flavors before using.

2 To make the *salsa verde,* in a blender, combine the tomatillos, garlic, chile, onion, and cilantro. Process well but not until completely smooth; the sauce should have a little texture to it. Transfer to a bowl, season to taste with salt, and thin, if necessary, with a little water.

3 Line a large platter with crushed ice. To shuck, or open, the oysters, use a stainless-steel oyster knife. Protect the hand that will hold the oysters with a folded towel. Working with 1 oyster at a time, hold it in your hand, with the top shell (the flatter, as opposed to the more bowl-shaped, shell) facing upward, the rounded end of the oyster near your thumb, and the pointed, or hinged end, toward you. Insert the knife tip into the hinge and turn it forcefully upward to break the hinge. Then, slip the knife blade along the inside surface of the top shell to sever the muscle that attaches it. Be careful not to pierce the oyster, or to tip the shell and lose the liquor. Lift off the top shell and discard. Now, run the knife under the oyster to separate it from the muscle. Place the oyster on the ice-lined platter and repeat with the remaining oysters. Nestle the salsa bowls in the ice and serve.

Serve with a chilled ale or a light, fruity white wine such as Sauvignon Blanc.

FOR THE SALSA CRUDA

2 ripe yet firm tomatoes, cored, halved, seeded (page 187), and finely diced

½ large white onion, finely minced

1 serrano chile, or more to taste, finely minced

1½ tablespoons chopped fresh cilantro (fresh coriander)

1½ teaspoons fresh lime juice, or more to taste

Fine sea salt

FOR THE SALSA VERDE

½ lb (250 g) tomatillos, husked, rinsed well, and quartered through the stem end

1 clove garlic

1 serrano chile

¼ white onion, coarsely chopped

1 tablespoon chopped fresh cilantro (fresh coriander)

Fine sea salt

Crushed ice for lining platter

36 oysters

Makes 6 servings

Swan Oyster Depot

Faced with a craving for fresh oysters, many San Franciscans head for Swan on Polk Street. A combination fish market–oyster bar, the venerable Swan has outlasted many trendier, more ambitious spots. The five Sancimino brothers who run it, sons of the Sicilian fisherman who bought it in the 1940s, know better than to mess with their formula. Their twenty stools are occupied all day with fans of impeccably fresh seafood.

Take a seat at the marble counter and order a half-dozen oysters and a glass of white wine. Spread some sweet butter on a chunk of sourdough bread and watch the countermen slice smoked salmon or wrap up some fresh wild salmon for a customer's dinner. Follow your oysters with some of that velvety smoked salmon or Swan's famous crab Louis. In a town renowned for cutting-edge cooking, Swan is endearingly retro.

In Swan's early years, native Olympia oysters were surely among its attractions. But that wild population has been lost to poor water quality, and today farms such as Hog Island in Tomales Bay provide San Franciscans with cultured oysters.

STEAMED SHRIMP DUMPLINGS

These delicate, open-faced dumplings resemble siu mai, *among the most popular offerings in the Bay Area's dim sum establishments. Virtually every restaurant serves* siu mai, *and most diners would consider their Chinese tea lunch incomplete without them. The traditional filling includes ground (minced) pork and shrimp, but this version puts the accent on shrimp. Note that you will need a flat-bottomed steamer, such as a Chinese bamboo steamer, for this dish. You will also need a small amount of pork fat; ask a butcher for trimmings or reserve your own. The round, extra-thin* siu mai *wrappers are available in Chinese markets.*

¾ lb (12 oz / 375 g) large shrimp (prawns), peeled and deveined (page 187)

1 oz (30 g) pork fat, diced

4 fresh water chestnuts, peeled and quartered

2 green (spring) onions, white and pale green parts only, sliced

3 fresh ginger slices, each ⅛ inch (3 mm) thick, peeled

1 large clove garlic, sliced

1 tablespoon dry sherry

1 tablespoon cornstarch (cornflour)

Fine sea salt

½ teaspoon sugar

½ teaspoon Asian sesame oil

1 egg white

30 *siu mai* wrappers, 3 inches (7.5 cm) in diameter

FOR THE DIPPING SAUCE

½ cup (4 fl oz/125 ml) soy sauce

Chile oil

Makes 6 servings

1 In a food processor, combine the shrimp, pork fat, water chestnuts, green onions, ginger, garlic, sherry, cornstarch, 1½ teaspoons salt, sugar, sesame oil, and egg white. Process until smooth.

2 Line a baking sheet with parchment (baking) paper. Work with 1 *siu mai* wrapper at a time, and keep the others covered with a towel to prevent them from drying out. Place the wrapper on a work surface and put about 1 tablespoon filling in the center of it. With both hands, lift the wrapper and use your thumbs and fingertips to cup the wrapper around the filling without enclosing it, pleating the wrapper like a cupcake liner at 8 equidistant points. Set the dumpling on the fingertips of one hand to flatten the bottom, then wrap the thumb and index finger of your other hand around the dumpling and press gently to make a "waist," flatten the pleats, and help the wrapper adhere to the filling. Set the dumpling on the prepared baking sheet. Repeat with the remaining filling and wrappers.

3 In a wok or other pot in which your steamer rests snugly in the rim, pour in water to a depth of 1 inch (2.5 cm) and bring to a boil over high heat. Lightly oil the bottom of the steamer and arrange the dumplings inside, not touching and filling side up—you may need to steam them in 2 batches—top with the lid, and set the steamer over the boiling water. Reduce the heat to medium and steam until the filling is firm and the wrapper is cooked, 10–20 minutes, replenishing the boiling water as needed.

4 While the dumplings steam, make the dipping sauce. In a small bowl, stir together the soy sauce with chile oil to taste. Divide among 6 dipping saucers, if you have them, or pass the dipping sauce in a cruet.

5 Bring the dumplings to the table in the steamer and serve at once with the dipping sauce.

Serve with an off-dry white wine such as Riesling or Gewürztraminer.

GRILLED ASPARAGUS WITH PARMESAN AND ORANGE-FLAVORED OLIVE OIL

Inspired by some Tuscan producers, a few California olive oil manufacturers make specialty oils by crushing the olives with a variety of citrus. On gourmet market shelves, you can find oils scented with lime, lemon, orange, blood orange, and more. Grilled asparagus with orange oil is one particularly successful match. The asparagus are blanched first, then seared on a hot grill. California's prime asparagus growing areas—the San Joaquin Valley and Salinas Valley—are close enough to San Francisco that the spears are generally pristine when they arrive. Spears range from pencil-thin to jumbo and are equally tender.

1 Holding an asparagus spear between both hands, nearer the lower end of the spear, bend it until it snaps naturally at the point at which the spear becomes tough. Discard the tough end. Repeat with the remaining spears.

2 Bring a large pot three-fourths full of water to a boil over high heat. Salt the boiling water, then add the asparagus spears and boil just until they lose their raw taste, 1½–2 minutes for medium-sized spears. Drain, then plunge in a bowl of ice water to stop the cooking. Drain again and pat dry on kitchen towels.

3 Prepare a charcoal or gas grill for direct grilling over high heat. If the grill rack is adjustable, position it about 3 inches (7.5 cm) from the fire.

4 Coat the asparagus spears evenly with the extra-virgin olive oil and season with sea salt. Place them on the grill rack, laying them across the bars. Cook until blistered and lightly charred on the underside, then turn them with tongs and cook until the other side is blistered and lightly charred. The total cooking time is 3–5 minutes, depending on the heat of the fire.

5 Transfer the asparagus to a serving platter. Drizzle with the orange olive oil and toss gently. Using a vegetable peeler or cheese plane, shave 2 oz (60 g) of cheese as thinly as possible over the asparagus. Toss again gently so as not to break up the shards too much. Serve at once.

Serve with a light white wine such as Sauvignon Blanc or a dry sherry.

2 lb (1 kg) asparagus

Fine sea salt

1 tablespoon extra-virgin olive oil

1½ teaspoons orange-flavored olive oil

Wedge of Parmigiano-Reggiano cheese

Makes 4 servings

ARTICHOKE AND LEEK FRITTATA

Maneuvering past the floor stacks of olive oil and shelves crammed with dried imported pasta, shoppers in San Francisco's Italian delis can always count on finding thick frittatas ready to be sliced for the customer on the go. A frittata is easy to make at home, requiring less dexterity than an omelet and allowing more leisurely timing. What's more, frittatas are just as good at room temperature as they are straight from the pan. Leftover fritatta, sliced and layered in a baguette with a little mayonnaise, makes a wonderful sandwich. The artichoke farms in nearby Monterey County harvest much of the year, but spring is peak season.

Juice of 1 lemon

8 baby artichokes, about 2 oz (60 g) each

Fine sea salt and freshly ground pepper

2 tablespoons unsalted butter

2 cups (6 oz/185 g) thinly sliced leeks, white and pale green parts only (2 to 3 medium-sized leeks)

6 eggs

¼ cup (1 oz/30 g) grated Parmesan cheese

2 tablespoons minced fresh flat-leaf (Italian) parsley

Makes 4 servings

1 Fill a bowl with cold water and add the lemon juice. Working with 1 artichoke at a time, peel back the tough outer leaves until they break off at the base. Keep removing leaves until you reach the tender, pale green heart. Cut about ¼ inch (6 mm) off the top of the heart to remove the pointed leaf tips. Pare the stem and trim the base to remove any dark green parts. Immediately drop the trimmed hearts into the lemon water to prevent browning.

2 Bring a pot three-fourths full of water to a boil over high heat. Salt the boiling water, then drain the trimmed artichoke hearts and add them to the boiling water. Boil until tender when pierced with a knife, 5–7 minutes. Drain and transfer to a bowl of ice water; when cool, drain again. Cut the artichokes in half lengthwise, then cut lengthwise into slices ¼ inch (6 mm) thick. Pat them dry.

3 In a 10-inch (25-cm) flameproof nonstick frying pan over medium-low heat, melt the butter. Add the leeks and cook, stirring occasionally, until soft, 10–12 minutes. Stir in the artichokes, season with salt and pepper, and cook the vegetables together for 2 minutes to infuse them with the seasoning.

4 In a bowl, whisk together the eggs, Parmesan, and parsley just until blended. Add the egg mixture to the pan and stir for just a few seconds to distribute the vegetables evenly. Reduce the heat to low and cook slowly, uncovered, until the eggs are almost completely set, 15–20 minutes. The eggs may still be a little moist in the center.

5 While the eggs are cooking, preheat the broiler (grill) and position a rack about 8 inches (20 cm) from the heat source. When the eggs are ready, slip the pan in the broiler and broil (grill) until the top is lightly colored and the center is firm to the touch. Remove from the broiler and, using a rubber or silicone spatula, loosen the edges of the frittata, and then slide it carefully onto a serving platter. Serve warm, not hot; cut into wedges.

Serve with a light white wine such as a Chenin Blanc or with a sparkling wine.

SALMON TARTARE WITH CRÈME FRAÎCHE AND SALMON ROE

The king (Chinook) salmon caught off the Northern California coast in summer are considered by many to be the tastiest salmon species. Certainly Bay Area cooks and diners look forward every year to the arrival of this local specialty. Although many cooks wouldn't consider any preparation other than grilling, these prized fish, with their high fat content, make a richly flavorful tartare—a raw dish inspired by the classic steak tartare. If wild salmon is not in season or is unavailable, you can make this dish with farmed salmon.

1 To make the dressing, in a small bowl, whisk together the crème fraîche, lemon juice, shallot, and Cognac. Season to taste with salt and pepper.

2 Ask your fishmonger to bone and skin the salmon fillet, or you can do it yourself: Using needle-nosed pliers, pull the slender pin bones from the fillet. (You can feel them by running your fingers across the surface.) Working from the side of the fillet, slide a sharp, thin knife between the skin and flesh of the fish. Grasp the skin in one hand and pull gently as you slide the knife underneath the flesh to remove the skin.

3 Using a sharp knife, cut the salmon into neat ¼-inch (6-mm) dice. Transfer to a chilled bowl, add the dressing, and toss gently.

4 Divide the salmon among chilled individual plates. Garnish each portion with 1 tablespoon salmon roe and a sprinkle of chives. Serve at once.

Serve with a dry sparkling wine or Champagne.

Note: Wild Pacific salmon may harbor tiny roundworms that can cause illness unless the fish is thoroughly cooked. Smart shoppers buy only from top-quality merchants whose suppliers clean the fish quickly after landing, a practice that minimizes—but doesn't eliminate—the risk. Always visually inspect king salmon thoroughly before using it for tartare.

FOR THE DRESSING

5 tablespoons (2½ oz/75 g) crème fraîche (page 185)

2 tablespoons fresh lemon juice

1 large shallot, finely minced

1 tablespoon Cognac or brandy

Fine sea salt and coarsely cracked pepper

¾ lb (375 g) salmon fillet, well chilled

¼ cup (3 oz/90 g) salmon roe

2 tablespoons thinly sliced fresh chives

Makes 4 servings

Sparkling Wines

Until the 1980s, California sparkling wine was not a beverage that wine lovers took seriously; connoisseurs bought French Champagne. Today, thanks to several pioneers, California sparklers compete on the world stage. In tastings, they often beat their French counterparts.

In Napa Valley, Jack and Jamie Davies launched California's sparkling-wine revolution with their 1965 Schramsberg Blanc de Blancs made from Chardonnay grapes. (The state's sparkling wines were previously made with less distinguished varietals.) Subsequently, several French firms established operations in California—among them, Champagne Taittinger (Domaine Carneros), Moet et Chandon (Domaine Chandon), and Champagne Roederer (Roederer Estate). And more American producers, such as Iron Horse and J Wine Company, followed the Davieses in targeting quality. All these producers use the *méthode champenoise,* which depends on a second fermentation in the bottle to produce the bubbles. With this painstaking process and cool-climate grapes, vintners have validated California's potential for fine sparkling wine.

BRUSCHETTA WITH CHERRY TOMATOES

One sign of the Bay Area's kinship with Italy is the enthusiasm with which locals have embraced bruschetta, *the thick-sliced appetizer toasts topped with all manner of savory ingredients. A few may mispronounce it (it's brew-SKET-ta), but restaurant diners know that* bruschette, *the plural, will get a meal off to a festive and informal start. Ripe, juicy tomatoes are the favored* bruschetta *topping in the Bay Area, where people are so passionate about tomatoes that many know the variety name of their favorites. With their petite size and candy-sweet flavor, Sweet 100 and Sungold cherry tomatoes have a particularly avid fan club.*

½ lb (250 g) small cherry tomatoes, preferably red and gold, halved or quartered

2 tablespoons extra-virgin olive oil

Fine sea salt and freshly ground pepper

½ cup (4 oz/125 g) whole-milk ricotta cheese

6 slices dense, day-old coarse country bread, each about 4 inches (10 cm) long, 3 inches (7.5 cm) wide, and ½ inch (12 mm) thick

1 clove garlic, halved

1 tablespoon chopped fresh basil

Makes 6 servings

1 Prepare a charcoal or gas grill for direct grilling over medium heat. Alternatively, preheat the broiler (grill).

2 In a bowl, combine the cherry tomatoes and olive oil. Season to taste with salt. Let stand for about 30 minutes to draw out some of the tomato juices.

3 In a small bowl, whisk the ricotta until smooth. Season to taste with salt and pepper.

4 Place the bread slices on the grill rack and grill, turning them once, until golden on both sides. Alternatively, place the bread slices on a baking sheet and toast under the broiler (grill), turning once, until golden on both sides. Remove from the grill or broiler and immediately rub 1 side of each slice with the cut sides of the halved garlic clove.

5 Divide the ricotta among the toasts, spreading it in an even layer. Stir the basil into the tomatoes, then spoon the tomatoes and any juices over the bread. Serve at once.

Serve with a crisp white wine such as Sauvignon Blanc or Pinot Grigio.

QUESADILLAS WITH CHORIZO AND JACK CHEESE

The taquerías that thrive in San Francisco's Mission District and along Oakland's International Boulevard draw a multicultural clientele. The fat burritos, soft tacos, and quesadillas satisfy diners looking for lunch on the run or an inexpensive but tasty meal. The version below uses Mexican chorizo, an uncured pork sausage seasoned with dried chiles and vinegar, and Monterey jack cheese or queso Oaxaca, a Mexican-style cheese similar to mozzarella. Add sliced pickled jalapeño chiles for an extra bit of heat, or replace the chorizo with strips of roasted Anaheim chiles for a delicious vegetarian variation.

1 In a frying pan over medium-low heat, fry the chorizo, breaking it up with a fork, until the meat is cooked through, 5–10 minutes. Drain the chorizo in a sieve, discarding the fat. Taste the chorizo; if it is not spicy enough for your taste, transfer it to a bowl and stir in chipotle chile to taste.

2 Place a 12-inch (30-cm) frying pan over medium heat. Add 1 teaspoon of the canola oil and swirl to coat the pan. When the oil is hot, place a tortilla in the pan. Sprinkle half of the surface (a half-moon) with one-fourth of the cheese, taking care to keep the cheese away from the edges so it doesn't melt in the pan. Top the cheese with one-fourth of the chorizo and 2 tablespoons of the cilantro. Fold the uncovered half of the tortilla over the filling, press gently, then move the folded tortilla into the center of the pan. Cook until nicely browned on the bottom, about 30 seconds. Using tongs or a spatula, carefully flip the quesadilla and cook on the second side until it is nicely colored and the cheese has melted, 30–60 seconds longer.

3 Transfer to a cutting board, cut into wedges, and serve piping hot. Repeat with the remaining ingredients, adding 1 teaspoon of the oil to the pan before adding each tortilla.

Serve with margaritas.

½ lb (250 g) Mexican chorizo, casing removed

Finely minced chipotle chile in adobo sauce (optional)

4 teaspoons canola or vegetable oil

4 flour tortillas, each about 9 inches (23 cm) in diameter

½ lb (250 g) Monterey jack cheese or *queso Oaxaca*, shredded

½ cup (¾ oz/20 g) coarsely chopped fresh cilantro (fresh coriander)

Makes 4 servings

ROASTED PEPPERS WITH CAPERS AND ANCHOVIES

Summer winds down at Bay Area farmers' markets in a burst of color, as bell peppers ripen into splendid hues of scarlet, orange, and gold. At some markets, a vendor chars them over an open flame, perfuming the air with their smoky smell. Peeled and sliced, the meaty peppers soak up the flavors of their dressing—in this case, a vinaigrette with anchovies and capers. Serve as a first course or as an accompaniment to roast chicken or grilled swordfish, and provide crusty bread to soak up the juices. Look for peppers that feel heavy, which indicates that they are fleshy. Avoid any with soft spots or shriveled skin.

6 large, thick-walled bell peppers (capsicums), preferably 2 *each* red, yellow (or gold), and green

2 tablespoons extra-virgin olive oil

1 large clove garlic, finely minced

6 meaty anchovy fillets, minced to a paste

1½ tablespoons salt-packed capers, rinsed, patted dry, and chopped

2 teaspoons sherry vinegar

Fine sea salt

Makes 4 servings

1 Preheat the broiler (grill). Line a baking sheet with aluminum foil for easy cleanup.

2 Arrange the peppers on the prepared baking sheet. Slip them under the broiler about 6 inches (15 cm) from the heat source. Broil (grill), turning as needed, until blackened on all sides. Set aside until cool enough to handle, then peel, removing all traces of charred skin. Do not rinse the peppers. Halve and remove the stem, seeds, and ribs, then cut the peppers lengthwise into strips about ½ inch (12 mm) wide, capturing any juices. Put the peppers and the juices in a bowl.

3 In a large frying pan over medium-low heat, warm the olive oil. Add the garlic and sauté briefly to release its fragrance. Add the peppers and their juices. Toss to coat with the seasoning and cook until they are hot throughout, about 2 minutes. Stir in the anchovies and the capers and remove from the heat.

4 Transfer to a serving dish, let cool briefly, then stir in the vinegar and season to taste with salt. Serve the peppers at room temperature.

Serve with a dry rosé.

MARINATED OLIVES WITH GARLIC, THYME, AND ORANGE ZEST

In Napa and Sonoma counties, olive trees are an increasingly popular landscape element. Many people plant olives around a new home to create a Mediterranean ambience; others inherit mature trees. Curing the harvest in late fall becomes an annual ritual, yielding beautiful jars of glistening olives to give as gifts or open for guests. Those who don't have their own olive crop can make the most of store-bought olives with this aromatic marinade. A mix of green and black olives is prettiest, but any varieties that have not been seasoned will work.

1 In a bowl, combine the olives, olive oil, garlic, thyme, and orange zest. Stir well, then cover and let marinate at room temperature for 24–36 hours, stirring occasionally.

2 Serve the olives at room temperature. They will keep, refrigerated, for several days, but bring to room temperature before serving.

Serve with a spicy red wine such as Zinfandel or a dry rosé.

¾ cup (4 oz/125 g) Picholine olives

¾ cup (4 oz/125 g) Niçoise olives

⅓ cup (3 fl oz/80 ml) extra-virgin olive oil

1 clove garlic, finely minced

1 teaspoon minced fresh thyme

¾ teaspoon grated orange zest

Makes 6 servings

Wine Bars

For wine lovers, San Francisco is arguably the best city in the world. International wines are well represented in wine shops and restaurants, and the selection of California wines is second to none. This unparalleled wealth of choice is displayed nightly at the city's wine bars. These establishments offer an opportunity to sample hard-to-find wines, older bottles, or selections unaffordable except by the glass. Wine bars regularly organize "flights," or comparative tastings, to allow patrons to compare, for example, four Rieslings from different countries.

At EOS Wine Bar, the wine manager orchestrates ten different flights each week, such as a sparkling wine flight and a "big, juicy reds" flight. First Crush, near Union Square, claims to have the largest all-California wine list in the city. Bacar, in the SoMa District, is famed for its wall of wine (seen above). The London Wine Bar in San Francisco's Financial District, opened in 1974, boasts that it is America's oldest wine bar, with about two dozen wines by the glass. And at Hayes & Vine, the wine list includes over twelve hundred choices.

SOUPS AND SALADS

With farm-fresh produce and fruits of the sea within reach year-round,

Bay Area cooks like soups and salads that speak of the season.

San Franciscans admire soups and salads that show the cook's imagination and respect for local produce and seafood. Bay Area salads are often strikingly colorful, whether a simple mix of sliced heirloom tomatoes with crumbled blue cheese or an artful composition of beets, fennel, avocado, and ricotta salata. Easy access to an extraordinary range of seasonal greens inspires such pairings as mesclun (mixed baby lettuces) with warm goat cheese or chicories with blood oranges and fennel. Soups also change with the seasons, showcasing tomatoes in summer, butternut squash in autumn, and the prized Dungeness crab in a hearty winter cioppino.

FARMERS' MARKET GREENS WITH BAKED GOAT CHEESE TOASTS

Warm baked goat cheese on a bed of baby lettuces is one dish that never leaves the Chez Panisse Café menu. Although goat cheese is commonplace now, it was a novelty in the early 1980s when Laura Chenel, a novice Sonoma County cheese maker, approached Chez Panisse proprietor Alice Waters with samples of her fresh goat cheese. Waters immediately placed a standing order, and Chenel has since become one of America's leading goat cheese producers. The relationship exemplifies Chez Panisse's longstanding support for local farmers and food producers.

1 To make the vinaigrette, in a small bowl, combine the vinegar, shallot, and a generous pinch of salt and let stand for 30 minutes to allow the shallot flavor to mellow. Whisk in the olive oil. Season to taste with pepper and with more salt if needed.

2 Preheat the oven to 425°F (220°C). Brush the baguette slices on both sides with about 1 tablespoon of the olive oil. Bake until they are nicely browned, 6–8 minutes. Set aside to cool. They will crisp as they cool. Reduce the oven temperature to 350°F (180°C).

3 Lightly oil a small baking dish and put the goat cheese in it. Sprinkle with the thyme, and drizzle with the remaining 1½ teaspoons olive oil. Bake until the goat cheese is soft and quivery to the touch, about 10 minutes.

4 While the goat cheese bakes, in a bowl, toss the salad greens with the vinaigrette. Taste and adjust the seasoning. Divide the greens among individual salad plates. If using edible flowers, divide and scatter them evenly over the greens.

5 Spread the warm cheese on the toasts, dividing it evenly. Arrange 3 toasts on each plate and serve the salads at once.

Serve with a light, chilled white wine such as Chenin Blanc or Fumé Blanc.

FOR THE VINAIGRETTE

1 tablespoon Champagne vinegar

1 shallot, finely minced (about 2 tablespoons)

Fine sea salt and freshly ground pepper

3 tablespoons extra-virgin olive oil

12 thin, diagonally cut slices baguette

1½ tablespoons extra-virgin olive oil

¼ lb (125 g) fresh goat cheese without a rind, at room temperature

1 teaspoon coarsely chopped fresh thyme

6 oz (185 g) mixed baby salad greens

About ½ cup (1 oz/30 g) loosely packed unsprayed edible flowers such as nasturtiums, marigolds, or chive blossoms (optional)

Makes 4 servings

BUTTERNUT SQUASH SOUP WITH CHIPOTLE CHILES AND CREMA

Sonoma County's scenic Alexander Valley lures many weekend cyclists and wine tasters, some of whom pause for refreshment at the retro Jimtown Store near Healdsburg. Owner Carrie Brown makes imaginative sandwiches and soups, including a Latin-inflected butternut squash soup that inspired this one. Healdsburg has a large Latino population, so it's not surprising that ingredients like chipotle chiles and Mexican crema have worked their way into many local kitchens. You can find crema in any Mexican market. Similar to crème fraîche, it is thickened, cultured cream with a slight tang. Sour cream is an acceptable substitute.

1 butternut squash, 3 lb (1.5 kg)

3 tablespoons olive oil

1 teaspoon cumin seeds

1 large white onion, minced

2 large cloves garlic, minced

5 cups (40 fl oz/1.25 l) light chicken stock, or equal parts canned reduced-sodium chicken broth and water, plus more if needed

½–1 chipotle chile in adobo sauce, very finely minced

Fine sea salt

½ cup (4 oz/125 g) *crema* or sour cream

¼ cup (⅓ oz/10 g) coarsely chopped fresh cilantro (fresh coriander)

Makes 6–8 servings

1 Preheat the oven to 375°F (190°C). Cut the squash into 8 roughly equal pieces, and remove the cavity seeds and strings. Using 1 tablespoon of the olive oil, coat a baking dish large enough to hold all the squash pieces in a single layer. Put the squash pieces in the baking dish, cut side down. Cover and bake until tender when pierced with the tip of a knife, about 50 minutes. Let cool completely.

2 In a small, dry frying pan over medium-low heat, toast the cumin seeds until fragrant and beginning to darken, about 5 minutes. Pour into a mortar and pound until finely ground with a pestle.

3 In a large pot over medium-low heat, warm the remaining 2 tablespoons oil. Add the onion and sauté, stirring often, until softened, about 10 minutes. Add the garlic and cumin and sauté briefly to release the garlic fragrance.

4 While the onion is cooking, scrape the squash flesh from the skins. Add the squash to the pot along with the 5 cups stock. Stir in the chile to taste; you will probably use less than a whole one. Bring the mixture to a simmer over medium heat, adjust the heat to maintain a gentle simmer, and cook for 5 minutes to blend the flavors.

5 In a food processor, in batches, purée the soup until completely smooth. Pour the soup into a clean pan and place over medium heat. Reheat to serving temperature, thinning if desired with more stock or with water. Season to taste with salt.

6 Divide the soup among warmed individual bowls. Whisk the *crema* with enough water to make it thin enough to drizzle, then drizzle some over each serving. Garnish with the cilantro and serve at once.

Serve with an off-dry white wine such as Riesling or a light-bodied beer.

CRACKED CRAB WITH MEYER LEMON VINAIGRETTE

San Franciscans are as devoted to the West Coast's Dungeness crab as Maine residents are to lobster. The local catch usually peaks in December and January, just in time for holiday tables. Although many markets carry freshly cooked Dungeness crab, purists boil their own. Some people use only salted water; others flavor the liquid with vegetables and seasonings. The crabs are delicious straight from the pot, but a leisurely bath in a marinade does them no harm. Meyer lemons give the marinade a particularly compelling fragrance, but you can substitute familiar Eureka lemons. The latter are more tart, so you will need less juice.

1 To make the court bouillon, combine the onions, celery, carrot, bay leaf, peppercorns, salt, wine, and 8 qt (8 l) water in a large pot. Bring to a boil over high heat, reduce the heat to maintain a steady simmer, and cook, uncovered, for 20 minutes.

2 While the court bouillon is simmering, make the marinade: In a large bowl, whisk together the olive oil, lemon juice, parsley, and garlic. Season to taste with salt.

3 Return the court bouillon to a boil over high heat. Add the crabs, cover, and cook for 20 minutes (less if your crabs are smaller than 2 lb) after the liquid returns to a boil. Lift them out of the boiling liquid and set aside to cool.

4 Twist off the crab claws and legs and set them aside. Holding each crab from underneath, lift off and discard the hard top shell. Turn the crab over; lift off and discard the triangular tail flap. Pull off and discard the grayish feathery gills along both sides.

5 With a heavy knife or a cleaver, quarter the body. If necessary, rinse the body pieces very quickly to remove the yellowish "butter." Gently crack the claws and legs with a nutcracker or mallet and put them in the marinade along with the quartered body. Stir well with a spatula and let marinate at room temperature for 1 hour, stirring occasionally.

6 Alternatively, cover and refrigerate the crab for up to 8 hours, stirring occasionally.

7 Serve the crab at room temperature or, if it has been refrigerated, serve chilled. Provide a nutcracker for each diner and a bowl for the shells.

Serve with a rich, unoaked white wine such as Chardonnay or a French Chablis.

FOR THE COURT BOUILLON

2 yellow onions, halved and thinly sliced

2 celery stalks, cut into 1-inch (2.5-cm) chunks

1 carrot, cut into 1-inch (2.5 cm) chunks

1 bay leaf

12 peppercorns

½ cup (4 oz/125 g) fine sea salt

1 bottle (24 fl oz/750 ml) dry white wine

FOR THE MARINADE

½ cup (4 fl oz/125 ml) extra-virgin olive oil

¼ cup (2 fl oz/60 ml) fresh Meyer lemon juice

3 tablespoons minced fresh flat-leaf (Italian) parsley

1 large clove garlic, very finely minced

Fine sea salt

2 large live Dungeness crabs, about 2 lb (1 kg) each

Makes 4 servings

THAI HOT-AND-SOUR SOUP

San Francisco's innumerable Thai restaurants provide an inexpensive evening out. On a typical Friday night, Thai restaurants are packed with locals enjoying red curry duck, pad Thai (stir-fried noodles), green papaya salad, and other dishes they may think they could never reproduce. Hot-and-sour shrimp soup, a favorite, is on virtually every menu and, unlike some of the complex curries, is not difficult to make at home. Thanks to a profusion of local Asian markets, and to the sizable Asian-ingredient selection in many supermarkets, Bay Area residents don't have to go far to find ingredients essential to this aromatic soup.

¾ lb (375 g) large fresh shrimp (prawns), peeled and deveined (page 187), with tail segments intact and shells reserved

3 lemongrass stalks

5 thin slices galangal (page 186), about ¼ inch (6 mm) thick

3 fresh or dried kaffir lime leaves (page 62)

2 tablespoons Thai or Vietnamese fish sauce

⅓ lb (5 oz/155 g) fresh white mushrooms, brushed clean, stem ends trimmed, and caps quartered

1 tomato, peeled (page 187), cored, and cut into thin wedges

¼ small yellow onion, cut into thin lengthwise slivers

4 teaspoons Thai roasted chile paste (page 187)

2 small fresh red or green chiles such as Thai or serrano

¼ cup (2 fl oz/60 ml) fresh lime juice, or more to taste

¼ cup (⅓ oz/10 g) chopped fresh cilantro (fresh coriander)

Makes 6 servings

1 In a saucepan, combine the shrimp shells with 5 cups (40 fl oz/1.25 l) water. Discard the upper leafy part of each lemongrass stalk and cut off the tough end of the bulb. Remove the tough outer layer of the stalks. Cut the remainder into 1-inch (2.5-cm) lengths and smash them with a flat side of a heavy knife or cleaver blade. Add them to the saucepan. Bring to a simmer over medium heat, cover partially, and simmer gently for 15 minutes to create a flavorful stock. Remove from the heat and strain the stock through a fine-mesh sieve.

2 Pour the stock into a clean saucepan and add the galangal, lime leaves, fish sauce, mushrooms, tomato, onion, and chile paste. Remove the stems from the fresh chiles, then quarter the chiles lengthwise. Add as many of the quarters to the stock as you like; you may want to start with just a few.

3 Place the pan over medium heat, bring to a simmer, cover partially, and simmer gently until the mushrooms are barely tender, about 2 minutes. Taste halfway through and add more chile quarters if the soup is not spicy enough. Stir in the shrimp and simmer just until they turn pink, about 30 seconds. Remove from the heat.

4 Stir in the ¼ cup lime juice and the cilantro. Taste and adjust the seasoning with more lime juice. Ladle into warmed bowls and serve at once.

Serve with Thai beer such as Singha.

BEET, FENNEL, AND AVOCADO SALAD WITH RICOTTA SALATA

For many Bay Area chefs, Saturday morning begins with a trip to the Ferry Plaza Farmers' Market to get the pick of the week's harvest. Autumn through spring, beets are a highlight, especially the golden beets and pink-and-white-striped Chioggia beets. Chefs love these types because they don't "bleed" their color as red beets do, making possible many artful composed salads. In this one, crisp fennel and creamy avocado provide textural contrast with the beets, and thin shavings of ricotta salata add a salty counterpoint. This firm, white sheep's milk cheese from southern Italy is made by salting, pressing, and briefly aging ricotta.

1 Preheat the oven to 400°F (200°C). If the beet greens are still attached, cut them off, leaving 1 inch (2.5 cm) of the stem attached to avoid piercing the skin (leave the root attached as well). Save the greens for another use. Put the beets in a baking dish with water to a depth of ¼ inch (6 mm). Cover and bake until the beets are easily pierced with the tip of a knife, about 1 hour. Remove from the oven and, when cool enough to handle, peel the beets and trim the roots, then set aside to cool completely.

2 To make the vinaigrette, in a small bowl, combine the lemon juice, shallot, and a generous pinch of salt. Let stand for 30 minutes to allow the shallot flavor to mellow. Whisk in the olive oil. Season with pepper. Taste and adjust the seasoning.

3 Slice the cooled beets very thinly by hand. Put them in a bowl and toss gently with about one-third of the vinaigrette, taking care not to break up the slices. Make a thin bed of the beets on a large platter or divide evenly between individual plates.

4 Cut off the stems and feathery tops and any bruised outer stalks from the fennel bulb, then halve lengthwise. Using a mandoline, V-slicer, or sharp knife, slice each half crosswise paper-thin. Put the fennel in a bowl, add about one-half of the remaining vinaigrette, and toss to coat. Scatter the fennel over the beets. With a vegetable peeler or cheese plane, shave 1½ oz (45 g) ricotta salata evenly over the fennel. Alternatively, crumble the same amount of feta evenly over the fennel.

5 Using a large metal spoon, scoop the flesh of the avocado half from the peel in one piece. Put the avocado half cut side down on a work surface and thinly slice crosswise. Arrange the avocado slices attractively on top of the salad.

6 Drizzle the salad with as much of the remaining vinaigrette as desired (you may not need it all), then top with the parsley. Serve at once.

Serve with a lean, lemony white wine such as Sauvignon Blanc.

4 beets, preferably golden or Chioggia, about 1 lb (500 g) total weight without greens

FOR THE VINAIGRETTE

1½ tablespoons fresh lemon juice

1 shallot, finely minced (about 2 tablespoons)

Fine sea salt and freshly ground pepper

¼ cup (2 fl oz/60 ml) extra-virgin olive oil

1 small fennel bulb

Wedge of ricotta salata or feta cheese

½ large avocado

1 tablespoon minced fresh flat-leaf (Italian) parsley

Makes 4 servings

CIOPPINO WITH FOCACCIA TOASTS

In all likelihood, San Francisco's famous cioppino was born in the kitchens of Italian immigrant fishermen who were trying to re-create the fish soups from home. They had different seafood to work with, including the unparalleled Dungeness crab, but they preserved the Italian character of the dish. Today, cioppino appears mostly in seafood restaurants on San Francisco's wharf, but it is a superb invention worth making at home in crab season. You can vary the seafood you add to cioppino according to the market and your taste. Many cooks add clams, mussels, squid, or even swordfish if the price is right.

2 Dungeness crabs

1½ lb (750 g) lean fish bones

1 *each* large yellow onion, celery stalk, and carrot, coarsely chopped

2 fresh flat-leaf (Italian) parsley sprigs, plus chopped for garnish

1 bay leaf

12 black peppercorns

1 cup (8 fl oz/250 ml) *each* dry white wine and dry red wine

½ cup (4 fl oz/125 ml) plus 1½ tablespoons olive oil

2 cups (10 oz/315 g) *each* minced yellow onion, green bell pepper (capsicum), and celery

¼ lb (125 g) fresh white mushrooms, thinly sliced

4 large cloves garlic, minced

1 teaspoon dried oregano, crushed

½ teaspoon red pepper flakes

2 cans (28 oz/875 g each) plum (Roma) tomatoes with juice, puréed

Fine sea salt

8-inch (20-cm) square focaccia

16 large shrimp (prawns)

1½ lb (750 g) white fish fillets

Makes 8 servings

1 If using live crabs, cook, clean, and prepare the crabs as directed on page 105. With a heavy knife or a cleaver, quarter the body. Break the crab legs into sections. Gently crack the claws and legs with a nutcracker or mallet. Set aside until ready to use.

2 In a large pot, combine the fish bones; coarsely chopped onion, celery, and carrot; parsley sprigs; bay leaf; black peppercorns; white wine, and 8 cups (64 fl oz/2 l) water. Place over medium heat and bring to a simmer, skimming off any foam. Adjust the heat to maintain a gentle simmer and cook, uncovered, for 30 minutes. Remove from the heat and let cool. Line a fine-mesh sieve with cheesecloth (muslin), and place over a large bowl. Strain the stock through the sieve.

3 In a large pot over medium heat, warm the ½ cup olive oil. When the oil is hot, add the minced onion, bell pepper, and celery; mushrooms; garlic; oregano; and red pepper flakes. Sauté until the vegetables are softened, about 20 minutes, reducing the heat if necessary to keep them from browning. Add 4 cups (32 fl oz/1 l) of the stock, the tomatoes, the red wine, and salt to taste. Bring to a simmer, then adjust the heat to maintain a gentle simmer. Cook until the soup is tasty, about 30 minutes. Thin, if necessary, with additional stock. Reserve the remaining stock

for another use. (It will keep, well covered, in the refrigerator for up to 2 days or in the freezer for up to 1 month.)

4 While the soup simmers, make the focaccia toasts: Preheat the oven to 450°F (230°C). Cut the focaccia into 16 strips, each 1 inch (2.5 cm) wide and 4 inches (10 cm) long. Lightly brush the focaccia strips with the 1½ tablespoons olive oil, then arrange on a baking sheet. Bake until lightly toasted, about 5 minutes. Remove from the oven.

5 Peel the shrimp, leaving the tail segments intact, and devein (page 187). Cut the white fish fillets into ¾-inch (2-cm) cubes.

6 Just before serving the soup, stir in the shrimp and fish cubes. Simmer just until barely done, about 1 minute, then remove from the heat.

7 Divide the crab evenly among 8 warmed deep soup bowls. Ladle the soup into the bowls, again dividing evenly. Garnish with chopped parsley and serve at once. Pass the focaccia toasts separately.

Serve with a dry rosé or a light Italian white wine such as Pinot Grigio.

SPRING VEGETABLE SOUP WITH FAVA BEANS, LEEKS, AND PEAS

For many years, fresh fava beans were a closely held secret of San Francisco's Italian community. Shoppers had to go to North Beach to find them, and few non-Italians knew how to prepare them. Today, almost every restaurant with a Mediterranean focus showcases fava beans from spring through midsummer, or for as long as the chefs can get their hands on them. Taking a cue from the market, cooks often combine the bright green fava beans with other vegetables from the spring harvest, such as leeks and peas. In this delicate soup, a trio of fresh spring vegetables flavors a rich chicken stock lightly thickened with semolina.

1 Shell the fava beans, removing them from their fuzzy pods. Bring a saucepan three-fourths full of water to a boil over high heat. Add the beans and boil for 1 minute. Drain and immediately immerse in a bowl of ice water. When cool, drain again. Remove the outer skin of each bean by pinching open the end opposite the end that connected it to the pod. The peeled bean will slip out easily.

2 In a large saucepan over medium-low heat, warm the 2 tablespoons olive oil. Add the leeks, season with salt and pepper, and toss to coat with the oil. Cover and cook until softened but not colored, about 10 minutes, reducing the heat if needed to keep the leeks from browning. Add 5 cups (40 fl oz/1.25 l) of the chicken stock and bring to a simmer. Add the fava beans and peas and cook until they are slightly softened, 2 minutes or longer, depending on their size.

3 In a small bowl, whisk together the semolina and the remaining 1 cup (8 fl oz/250 ml) stock until smooth. Slowly add the semolina mixture to the soup while whisking constantly. Simmer gently, stirring often, until the semolina has lost its raw taste and the soup is slightly thickened, about 5 minutes.

4 Taste and adjust the seasoning. Ladle into warmed bowls and top each with a drizzle of olive oil.

Serve with a light Italian white wine such as Arneis or Fiano di Avellino.

2 lb (1 kg) fava (broad) beans

2 tablespoons extra-virgin olive oil, plus more for drizzling

1 cup (3 oz/90 g) thinly sliced leeks, white and pale green parts only

Fine sea salt and freshly ground pepper

6 cups (48 fl oz/1.5 l) rich chicken stock or canned reduced-sodium chicken broth

1½ lb (750 g) English peas, shelled

6 tablespoons (2 oz/60 g) semolina (page 187)

Makes 6 servings

MIXED WINTER CHICORIES WITH BLOOD ORANGES AND FENNEL

Most of California's blood orange cultivation is in the southern part of the state, where growers can count on mostly frost-free nights. But judging by markets and local menus, much of the harvest goes to the Bay Area, where it shows up in desserts and contemporary salads such as this one. Juicy blood oranges, bitter chicories, and crunchy sweet fennel make a memorable trio and are conveniently in season simultaneously, in the late winter months. The members of the chicory family—among them, escarole, radicchio, and frisée—perform best in cool weather and do well in coastal Northern California.

FOR THE VINAIGRETTE

2 tablespoons Champagne vinegar

1 large shallot, minced (about 2 tablespoons)

Fine sea salt and freshly ground pepper

5 tablespoons (2½ fl oz/75 ml) extra-virgin olive oil

1 head escarole

½ small head frisée

½ head radicchio

3 blood oranges

1 fennel bulb

2 tablespoons chopped fresh flat-leaf (Italian) parsley

Makes 6 servings

1 To make the vinaigrette, in a small bowl, combine the vinegar, shallot, and a generous pinch of salt and let the mixture stand for 30 minutes to allow the shallot flavor to mellow. Whisk in the olive oil and several grinds of pepper.

2 Remove the tough, dark outer escarole leaves and reserve for cooking. Tear the pale inner leaves into bite-sized pieces. Discard the tough, dark outer frisée leaves. Tear the tender inner leaves into bite-sized pieces. Cut the radicchio half into 2 wedges through the core, then cut away the core. Slice each wedge crosswise into narrow ribbons. Place the escarole, frisée, and radicchio in a large bowl.

3 Working with 1 orange at a time, and using a sharp knife, cut a slice off the top and bottom of the fruit, exposing the flesh. Place the orange upright on a cutting board and thickly cut off the peel in strips, removing all the peel and white pith underneath and

following the contour of the fruit. Holding the orange over a bowl, cut along either side of each section, freeing it from the membrane and allowing it to fall into the bowl.

4 Cut off the stems and feathery tops and any bruised outer stalks from the fennel bulb, then halve lengthwise. Using a mandoline, V-slicer, or sharp knife, slice each half crosswise paper-thin.

5 Add the fennel and parsley to the salad bowl. Using a slotted spoon, transfer the orange sections to the bowl as well, leaving any orange juices behind. Add the vinaigrette and toss well. Taste and adjust the seasoning, then serve at once.

Serve with an off-dry white wine such as a Riesling or Chenin Blanc.

HEIRLOOM TOMATO SALAD WITH BLUE CHEESE DRESSING

Tomato one-upmanship is virtually a summer sport in the San Francisco Bay Area, as markets compete to offer the most dramatic displays of colorful and unusual tomatoes. Many are heirloom types, prized generations ago for flavor and then almost forgotten in the modern embrace of tomatoes that ship and store well. Such fine tomatoes need no more than a sprinkle of sea salt or a classic vinaigrette, but a creamy dressing enriched with crumbled blue cheese, preferably the local Point Reyes Original Blue, provides a welcome alternative.

1 Core the large tomatoes and cut into wedges or slices. Cut cherry tomatoes in half. Arrange all the tomatoes attractively on a serving platter.

2 To make the dressing, in a small food processor or a blender, combine the mayonnaise, buttermilk, garlic, 2 teaspoons vinegar, and the blue cheese. Process until smooth. Transfer to a bowl and stir in salt to taste and more vinegar if desired.

3 In a small bowl, stir together the green onion and parsley, mixing well.

4 Drizzle the dressing over the tomatoes, using as much as you like (you may not need it all), then garnish with the green onion parsley mixture and several grinds of pepper. If desired, crumble extra blue cheese over the salad. Serve at once.

Serve with a light white wine such as Sauvignon Blanc or Pinot Grigio.

1½ lb (750 g) heirloom tomatoes, in a variety of sizes and colors

FOR THE DRESSING

¼ cup (2 fl oz/60 ml) mayonnaise, not low-fat

¼ cup (2 fl oz/60 ml) buttermilk

1 clove garlic, thinly sliced

2 teaspoons Champagne vinegar, or more to taste

2 oz (60 g) blue cheese (see Note), plus extra for crumbling

Fine sea salt

2 tablespoons minced green (spring) onion, white and pale green parts only

1 tablespoon minced fresh flat-leaf (Italian) parsley

Freshly ground pepper

Makes 4 servings

Heirloom Tomatoes

Every summer, Eatwell Farm's "Tomato Wonderland" delights shoppers at the San Francisco Ferry Plaza Farmers' Market. With dozens of varieties in shades of red, pink, orange, gold, yellow, purple, and green, the display makes a shopper want to pull out a salt shaker and feast on the spot.

Frances Andrews and Nigel Walker, Eatwell's owners, plant up to one hundred tomato varieties each year, many of them heirlooms. Cooks and gardeners seek out heirloom varieties for their superior flavor, and for the satisfaction of supporting the seed-saving movement.

Although no official definition of heirloom produce exists, most people use the word *heirloom* to describe varieties that have been handed down through generations. Some say a variety must be at least one hundred years old to qualify; others use the term for virtually any tomato that is not a modern hybrid.

Advocates of heirloom produce and seed saving believe it is important to preserve the world's genetic diversity. They worry that if commercial enterprises control the seed, some varieties may disappear.

MAIN COURSES

San Francisco restaurants introduce patrons to foreign ingredients and

exotic tastes, inspiring diners to try that five-spice chicken at home.

Local restaurants set the bar for Bay Area home cooks, who often try to re-create the ethnic dishes they've enjoyed while dining out. Homemade Vietnamese five-spice chicken comes remarkably close to the restaurant version, and any home cook can reproduce the slow-cooking method for salmon that Bay Area chefs have popularized. San Francisco's amateur cooks don't retreat to the familiar for main courses. Instead, they reach out to sample new tastes and master new techniques, such as searing tuna, brining pork chops, or producing a creamy risotto. Even the common hamburger gets reconceived with focaccia "buns."

DUNGENESS CRAB RISOTTO WITH LEMON AND PARSLEY

In November, the season opens on what is probably San Franciscans' favorite seafood: Dungeness crab. Fish markets and supermarkets sell it cooked and cleaned, but connoisseurs buy the crab live and cook their own. Cooking your own crab yields tastier meat than you can purchase cooked and cleaned, and it leaves you with crab shells with which to flavor a risotto stock. The best rice varieties for risotto are the medium-grain Italian types, such as Arborio, Carnaroli, and Vialone Nano. By adding hot liquid a little at a time, the grains gradually swell and soften. In a perfect risotto, all the grains are suspended in a creamy mass.

Fine sea salt and freshly ground pepper

1 live Dungeness crab, about 2 lb (1 kg)

2 cups (16 fl oz/500 ml) bottled clam juice

½ cup (4 fl oz/125 ml) dry white wine

1 large celery stalk, cut into 4 equal pieces

¼ yellow onion

5 tablespoons (2½ fl oz/75 ml) extra-virgin olive oil

1 cup (3 oz/90 g) thinly sliced leeks, white and pale green parts only

1½ cups (10½ oz/330 g) Arborio, Carnaroli, or Vialone Nano rice

2 tablespoons minced fresh flat-leaf (Italian) parsley

1 teaspoon grated lemon zest

Makes 4 servings

1 In a large pot over high heat, bring 8 qt (8 l) water to a boil. Salt the water generously—about 3 tablespoons for 8 qt. Add the live crab and cover the pot. Cook the crab for 20 minutes after the water returns to a boil, then lift the crab out of the water with tongs and set aside to cool.

2 Twist off the crab claws and legs and set them aside. Holding the crab from underneath, lift off the hard top shell. Rinse the top shell, pulling out any interior matter, and set the shell aside to add to the stock. Turn the crab over; lift off and discard the triangular tail flap. Pull off and discard the grayish feathery gills along both sides. With a heavy knife or a cleaver, quarter the body. If necessary, rinse the body pieces very quickly to remove the yellowish "butter."

3 Remove all the crabmeat from the body quarters, then crack the legs and claws and remove all the meat. Keep the meat in pieces as large as possible, and reserve all the shell pieces.

4 In a saucepan over medium heat, combine 4 cups (32 fl oz/1 l) water, the clam juice, wine, celery, onion, and crab shells. Bring to a simmer, adjust the heat to maintain a gentle simmer, and cook, uncovered, for 15 minutes. Place a fine-mesh sieve over a clean saucepan and strain the stock into the pan. Bring to a simmer over medium heat, then reduce the heat to keep it just below a simmer.

5 In a large saucepan over medium-low heat, warm 3 tablespoons of the olive oil. Add the leeks and stir to coat with the oil. Cook, stirring occasionally, until they are soft and sweet, 10–12 minutes. Add the rice and cook, stirring, until all the grains are hot. Begin adding the stock ½ cup (4 fl oz/125 ml) at a time, stirring often and adding more only when the previous addition has been absorbed. It should take about 20 minutes for the rice to become al dente and absorb most of the stock. (You may not need all of the stock.) The risotto should be creamy—neither soupy nor stiff—and the kernels should be tender yet firm in the center. Remove the risotto from the heat.

6 Set aside 4 attractive, large nuggets of crabmeat for garnish. Stir the remaining crabmeat into the rice along with the remaining 2 tablespoons olive oil, the parsley, and the lemon zest, distributing the ingredients. Season to taste with salt and pepper.

7 Spoon the risotto into warmed individual bowls, garnish each portion with one of the reserved nuggets of crabmeat, and serve at once.

Serve with a fine sparkling wine or a dry white wine from California's Mendocino County such as Riesling.

SLOW-ROASTED KING SALMON WITH BRAISED LENTILS

Baking salmon at a low temperature, a technique popular in Bay Area restaurants, produces a creamy, moist interior. Fillets of wild king salmon, a West Coast species with a high fat content, lend themselves well to this method, although you can also substitute farmed salmon. Here, the fillets are placed on a bed of buttery lentils and topped with a herb-shallot butter. Look for small French green lentils for this dish, not the larger brown type, which don't hold their shape as well. Lentils vary widely in their cooking times, so test often.

1 Preheat the oven to 300°F (150°C). Butter a baking dish large enough to hold the salmon in one layer.

2 To make the butter, in a bowl, combine the butter, shallot, parsley, and mustard and mix with a spoon until smooth. Season to taste with salt and pepper.

3 To cook the lentils, in a frying pan over medium-low heat, melt 2 tablespoons of the butter. Add the onion, carrot, celery, and garlic and sauté until softened, about 20 minutes. Meanwhile, in a saucepan over medium heat, combine the stock and thyme and bring to a simmer. Add the lentils, cover partially, and adjust the heat to maintain a simmer. Cook until the lentils are tender, 20–25 minutes. Remove from the heat and discard the thyme sprig. Using a slotted spoon, add the lentils to the vegetables along with a few tablespoons of their liquid. Season to taste with salt and pepper, stir well, then cover and simmer until the lentils have absorbed the liquid, about 10 minutes. Add more liquid if needed. Keep warm over low heat.

4 Season the salmon fillets on both sides with salt and pepper, then place in the prepared baking dish. Bake until the fish just flakes, 20–25 minutes.

5 Remove the lentils from the heat. Add the parsley and remaining butter and stir until the butter melts. Divide the lentils among warmed individual plates. Top with the salmon fillets, then top each fillet with herb butter, spreading it evenly. Serve at once.

Serve with a young, fruity red wine such as Pinot Noir.

FOR THE BUTTER

2 tablespoons unsalted butter, at room temperature

1 small shallot, finely minced

2 teaspoons minced fresh flat-leaf (Italian) parsley

1½ teaspoons Dijon mustard

Sea salt and freshly ground pepper

FOR COOKING THE LENTILS

3½ tablespoons unsalted butter

½ large yellow onion, minced

½ large carrot, peeled and diced

1 small inner celery stalk, diced

2 cloves garlic, minced

3 cups (24 fl oz/750 ml) light chicken stock, or equal parts canned reduced-sodium broth and water

1 large fresh thyme sprig

1 cup (7 oz/220 g) French green lentils, picked over and rinsed

Sea salt and freshly ground pepper

1½ tablespoons minced fresh flat-leaf (Italian) parsley

4 king salmon fillets, about 6 oz (185 g) each, skinned

Sea salt and freshly ground pepper

Makes 4 servings

Northern California's Pacific Catch

From winter's sweet Dungeness crab to summer's wild king salmon, local seafood is a precious resource that Bay Area diners treasure. Although air freight makes it easy to enjoy fish from afar, locals are loyal to their coastal catch.

In truth, little of the seafood in Bay Area markets and on menus is local by any strict definition. Only two fish—anchovies and herring—are commercially fished in San Francisco Bay in any quantity. However, boats that ply the Pacific between Monterey and Fort Bragg bring in plenty of sought-after seafood. Chief among them are three flatfish that are mainstays of local fish restaurants: sand dabs, petrale sole, and rex sole. Fresh sand dabs meunière, lightly dredged in flour and panfried with butter, lemon, and capers, are a memorable experience.

Pacific halibut appears in markets from late spring to fall. Chefs appreciate its adaptability, and diners like its mild taste. Monterey Bay yields abundant squid and sardines, and albacore tuna is a summer treat, making its way up the coast to the Bay Area as the ocean warms.

FOCACCIA BURGER WITH TOMATO, ARUGULA, AND AIOLI

Freshly ground, high-quality beef is essential to a good burger, of course, but the right bread is just as critical. Not content with conventional buns and, perhaps, hoping to distinguish their offering, some San Francisco restaurants have introduced the cross-cultural concept of a focaccia burger. The soft, yeasty flat bread is the perfect wrap for a hamburger. Liguria Bakery in North Beach has provided San Franciscans with focaccia for decades. If you don't have an Italian bakery nearby, check an Italian delicatessen for focaccia. This recipe yields more aioli than you need; save any leftover aioli for steamed artichokes.

FOR THE AIOLI

1 large clove garlic

Fine sea salt

1 egg yolk, at room temperature

½ cup (4 fl oz/125 ml) extra-virgin olive oil

1⅓ lb (655 g) ground (minced) beef chuck

Fine sea salt and freshly ground pepper

2 sheets thin plain focaccia, each 8 inches (20 cm) square, or 1 sheet thick plain focaccia, 8 inches square, halved horizontally

1 large tomato, cored and thinly sliced

½ red onion, very thinly sliced

1 large handful baby arugula (rocket), or larger arugula with stems removed

Makes 4 servings

1 To make the aioli, in a mortar, combine the garlic clove with a pinch of salt and pound to a paste with a pestle. Set aside. Put the egg yolk in a small bowl, add a few drops of warm water, and whisk to loosen the yolk. Begin whisking in the olive oil slowly—drop by drop at first, then a little faster once you see that you have achieved an emulsion. Whisk in the garlic paste. Taste and adjust with more salt if needed.

2 Season the meat with salt and pepper. Divide into 4 equal portions and shape each portion into a patty about 4 inches (10 cm) square and ½ inch (12 mm) thick.

3 Preheat the broiler (grill). Cut the focaccia sheets into 4-inch (10-cm) squares. Place on a baking sheet, slip into the broiler and toast, turning once, until lightly crisped on both sides.

4 Choose a frying pan, preferably nonstick, large enough to hold all the patties in a single layer without touching. Alternatively, use 2 frying pans. Place the pan(s) over medium heat. Add the patties, reduce the heat to medium-low, and cook until nicely browned on the bottom, about 3 minutes. Turn and cook to desired doneness, about 3 minutes longer for medium.

5 While the burgers are cooking, spread the bottom side or the cut side of each focaccia square with aioli. When the burgers are ready, immediately place a hot burger on 4 of the squares. Top each burger with tomato slices, a few slices of red onion, and several leaves of arugula. Cover with the remaining focaccia squares. Cut in half, if desired, and serve at once.

Serve with a full-bodied beer such as Amber or a spicy red wine such as Zinfandel.

STEAMED MUSSELS WITH SAFFRON AIOLI

Wild mussels cling to intertidal rocks along the Northern California coast, and adventurers armed with a fishing permit can harvest them in season (generally the colder months). But for day-to-day needs, most cooks rely on an easier source of supply: farmed mussels from Washington State or eastern Canada. Steaming them with saffron and orange zest and saucing them with aioli gives the mussels the Mediterranean accent that appeals to Bay Area diners. Serve family style with crusty bread to soak up the juices.

1 In a small bowl, combine the saffron and wine and leave to steep for 30 minutes.

2 To make the aioli, in a mortar, combine the garlic cloves with a pinch of salt and pound to a paste with a pestle. Set aside. Put the egg yolk in a small bowl, add a few drops of warm water, and whisk to loosen the yolk. Begin whisking in the olive oil slowly—drop by drop at first, then a little faster once you see that you have achieved an emulsion. Whisk in the garlic paste. Taste and adjust with more salt if needed.

3 Cut off the stems and feathery tops and any bruised outer stalks from the fennel bulb, then cut the bulb into ¼-inch (6-mm) dice.

4 In a large pot over medium-low heat, warm the olive oil. Add the fennel and shallot and sauté until the fennel is softened, 12–15 minutes. Add the mussels, discarding any that fail to close to the touch, along with the wine and saffron mixture and the orange zest. Raise the heat to high and bring to a boil. Boil, uncovered, for about 1 minute to drive off the alcohol, then cover and cook until the mussels open, shaking the pot occasionally, 3–4 minutes.

5 Whisk enough of the steaming juices into the aioli to make a sauce you can drizzle. Transfer the mussels and their juices to a serving bowl, discarding any mussels that failed to open. Remove and discard the orange zest strips, and drizzle the mussels with the aioli. Garnish with the parsley and serve at once.

Serve with a dry rosé or a Sauvignon Blanc.

¼ teaspoon powdered saffron, preferably saffron threads pounded in a mortar

1 cup (8 fl oz/250 ml) dry white wine

FOR THE AIOLI

2 cloves garlic

Fine sea salt

1 egg yolk, at room temperature

½ cup (4 fl oz/125 ml) extra-virgin olive oil

1 small fennel bulb

¼ cup (2 fl oz/60 ml) extra-virgin olive oil

¾ cup (4 oz/125 g) minced shallot

4 lb (2 kg) mussels, well scrubbed and beards removed

2 long orange zest strips

¼ cup (⅓ oz/10 g) chopped fresh flat-leaf (Italian) parsley

Makes 4 servings

Cooking Schools

With so many great ingredients in Bay Area markets and so many food-focused residents, it's not surprising that the region supports many cooking schools.

Several businesses offer single-session classes oriented to the home cook. At Draeger's supermarkets on the Peninsula, at Sur La Table in San Francisco and Berkeley, and at Ramekins in Sonoma, students can take classes on knife skills, Indian cooking, or chocolate desserts.

One of the oldest and most respected cooking schools in San Francisco is Tante Marie's, established in 1979 by Mary Risley. Still going strong, Risley's school offers courses for both amateurs and would-be professionals.

At least three schools in the Bay Area focus on building professional expertise. The program at City College of San Francisco trains participants for food-service jobs. At the California Culinary Academy in San Francisco, students master basic culinary skills, and in the Napa Valley, the Culinary Institute of America at Greystone offers continuing education for people working in the field.

BRINE-CURED PORK CHOPS WITH BALSAMIC GLAZE

Popularized by Bay Area meat expert Bruce Aidells and others, brining returns flavor and juiciness to modern pork bred for leanness. After only one day in a brine, thick pork chops are seasoned all the way through, not just on the surface. If not overcooked, they will be succulent beyond compare. The sugar in the brine also helps the chops brown beautifully. You can brine other lean cuts of pork as well, such as tenderloin or loin roasts. The thicker the muscle, the longer it will take for the brine to penetrate. Brined meats generally need no additional seasoning. Serve these chops with buttered Brussels sprouts or wilted spinach.

FOR THE BRINE

7 tablespoons (3½ oz/105 g) kosher or sea salt

¼ cup (2 oz/60 g) firmly packed brown sugar

½ bunch fresh thyme sprigs

4 cloves garlic, halved

1½ teaspoons coarsely cracked pepper

4 center-cut pork loin chops, each 1¼–1½ inches (3–4 cm) thick

1 tablespoon olive oil

2 tablespoons unsalted butter

¼ cup (1½ oz/45 g) minced shallot

2 tablespoons balsamic vinegar

1 cup (8 fl oz/250 ml) light chicken stock, or equal parts canned reduced-sodium chicken broth and water

1 tablespoon minced fresh sage

Makes 4 servings

1 To make the brine, in a saucepan over medium heat, combine the salt, brown sugar, thyme sprigs, garlic, pepper, and 8 cups (64 fl oz/2 l) water. Bring just to a simmer, stirring to dissolve the salt and sugar. Remove from the heat, and transfer the brine to a plastic or ceramic container large enough to hold both the pork chops and the brine. Let the brine cool completely, and then refrigerate until cold.

2 Add the pork chops to the cold brine, making sure they are submerged. If necessary, top the pork chops with a plate to weigh them down. Cover and refrigerate for 1 day.

3 Preheat the oven to 200°F (95°C). Remove the chops from the brine and pat them dry.

4 Choose a heavy frying pan large enough to hold all the chops in a single layer without touching. Place over medium-high heat until hot. Add the olive oil and swirl to coat the bottom. When the oil is hot, add the chops and reduce the heat to medium. Cook until nicely browned on the bottom, about 10 minutes, adjusting the heat if necessary to avoid scorching. Turn and cook until the chops are no longer pink at the bone, 10–12 minutes longer, spooning off excess fat as it accumulates. Transfer the chops to a heatproof platter and keep warm in the oven.

5 Pour off any fat in the frying pan and return to medium-low heat. Add 1 tablespoon of the butter. When the butter melts, add the shallot and cook, stirring, until softened, about 2 minutes. Add the vinegar, bring to a boil, and let boil briefly until reduced by half. Add the stock and sage, raise the heat to high, and boil, scraping up any browned bits on the pan bottom with a wooden spoon, until reduced to ⅓ cup (3 fl oz/ 80 ml). Remove from the heat, add the remaining 1 tablespoon butter, and swirl the pan without stirring until the butter melts.

6 Return the pan to low heat. Return the chops to the pan and cook gently for about 1 minute, turning them over in the sauce 2 or 3 times. Divide the chops among warmed individual plates, spooning any of the remaining sauce over each chop. Serve at once.

Serve with a light or medium-bodied red wine such as Pinot Noir or Sangiovese.

WINE-BRAISED SHORT RIBS WITH MUSHROOMS AND THYME

A rich and winy short-rib stew is the perfect antidote to one of San Francisco's wet, wintry nights. Often tough if cooked with dry heat, short ribs become tender and succulent when braised slowly with a small amount of liquid. This basic braise invites variation: substitute oxtails for the short ribs; add some chopped peeled tomato to the sautéed vegetables; or toss in a few dried porcini (ceps). Ask the butcher to cut the short ribs for you if necessary. The ribs can release a good amount of fat, so skim the sauce carefully. Serve with mashed potatoes.

1 Preheat the oven to 300°F (150°C). Season the ribs with salt and pepper. Place a large, heavy frying pan over high heat until hot. Add the olive oil and swirl to coat the bottom. When the oil is hot, add the meat, reduce the heat to medium, and brown well on all sides, about 25 minutes total. As the ribs are done, transfer them in a single layer to a large baking dish or pan.

2 Pour off all but 2 tablespoons fat in the frying pan and return to medium heat. Add the mushrooms, onion, carrot, celery, and thyme. Season with salt and pepper and cook, stirring occasionally, until the vegetables are softened, about 10 minutes. Transfer to the baking dish and return the empty pan to high heat. Add the wine and simmer until reduced by half, scraping up any browned bits with a wooden spoon. Add to the baking dish along with 1 cup (8 fl oz/250 ml) water. Cover lightly and bake until the ribs are fork-tender, 2½–3 hours. Remove from the oven.

3 Transfer the ribs to an ovenproof serving platter, cover with aluminum foil, and keep warm in the turned-off oven. Pour the contents of the baking dish into a large measuring pitcher and let settle for 5 minutes, then using a large spoon, skim off as much surface fat as possible. Pour the remainder into a frying pan and reheat to serve as a sauce. If the juices seem too thin, simmer over high heat to thicken and concentrate them. Taste and adjust the seasoning.

4 Pour the sauce over the ribs and garnish with the parsley. Serve at once.

Serve with a Carneros Pinot Noir (see right).

4 lb (2 kg) beef short ribs, cut into 3-inch (7.5-cm) lengths

Fine sea salt and freshly ground pepper

1 tablespoon olive oil

⅓ lb (5 oz/155 g) small fresh white mushrooms, brushed clean, trimmed, and quartered

½ large yellow onion, minced

1 large carrot, peeled and finely diced

1 large celery stalk, finely diced

1 tablespoon minced fresh thyme

1 cup (8 fl oz/250 ml) dry white wine

2 tablespoons minced fresh flat-leaf (Italian) parsley

Makes 4 servings

Carneros: Wine by the Bay

San Franciscans driving north across the Golden Gate Bridge for a day of wine tasting don't have to go far to find their first winery. The famed Carneros region, which straddles Napa and Sonoma counties, is only forty-five minutes away. It is home to some of the finest Pinot Noir, Chardonnay, and sparkling-wine producers in the state, among them Acacia, Artesa, Bouchaine, Buena Vista, Carneros Creek, Gloria Ferrer, Saintsbury, and Domaine Carneros.

For cool-climate grapes such as Pinot Noir and Chardonnay, Carneros is a near-ideal environment. The region's proximity to the Pacific Ocean and to San Pablo Bay, the northernmost part of San Francisco Bay, makes it one of California's coolest growing areas. Consequently, the grapes mature slowly, developing fruit flavors while maintaining their bracing acidity.

Pinot Noirs from the region tend to have a lovely perfume suggesting raspberries, cherries, clove, and berry jam. The Chardonnays show abundant fruit—think apples and pears—with crisp acidity to give them backbone.

ORECCHIETTE WITH BROCCOLI RABE

Southern Italians must feel right at home in San Francisco when they notice the widespread use of broccoli rabe (also known by its Italian name, cime di rapa) on local menus. A favorite in the regions of Campania and Apulia, the vegetable has countless Bay Area fans who have come to love its pleasing bitterness. Once relegated to Italian American markets, broccoli rabe has a secure niche in San Francisco supermarkets now. With its deep green florets, leaves, and stems, broccoli rabe looks like a broccoli cousin, but it's botanically closer to turnips. For another layer of flavor, add crumbled sausage or finely minced anchovies.

FOR THE BREAD CRUMBS

1 tablespoon extra-virgin olive oil

½ cup (2 oz/60 g) fine dried bread crumbs

Fine sea salt

1½ lb (750 g) broccoli rabe

Fine sea salt

1 lb (500 g) orecchiette

⅓ cup (3 fl oz/80 ml) extra-virgin olive oil

4 large cloves garlic, minced

Red pepper flakes

Makes 4–6 servings

1 To make the bread crumbs, in a small frying pan over medium-low heat, warm the olive oil. Add the bread crumbs and stir to coat them with the oil. Season lightly with salt and cook, stirring often, until the crumbs are an even, deep golden brown, about 10 minutes. Pour onto a plate and set aside to cool.

2 Bring a large pot three-fourths full of water to a boil over high heat.

3 Meanwhile, trim the broccoli rabe, removing any dry ends and any stems that feel tough. (With broccoli rabe, the thick stems tend to be tender; it's the spindly stems that may need removing.)

4 Salt the boiling water, then add the broccoli rabe and cook, testing often, until the stems are just tender, 2–3 minutes. Using tongs, a slotted spoon, or a wire-mesh skimmer, lift out the broccoli rabe and transfer it to a sieve, then cool it quickly under cold running water. Drain and squeeze gently to remove excess moisture. Chop coarsely and set aside.

5 Add the pasta to the boiling water, stir well, and cook until al dente, about 12 minutes, or according to the package directions.

6 While the pasta is cooking, in a large frying pan over medium-low heat, warm the olive oil. Add the garlic and the red pepper flakes to taste and sauté briefly to release the garlic fragrance. Add the broccoli rabe and season to taste with salt. Stir to coat with the seasoning. Cook until the broccoli rabe is hot throughout, about 2 minutes; keep warm.

7 When the pasta is ready, scoop out 1 cup (8 fl oz/250 ml) of the pasta water. Drain the pasta and return it to the pot. Add the broccoli rabe and stir well over low heat to combine, moistening the pasta if necessary with some of the reserved pasta water.

8 Divide the pasta among warmed individual plates or pasta bowls and top each portion with a sprinkling of the toasted bread crumbs. Pass the remaining bread crumbs at the table.

Serve with a light white wine such as Pinot Grigio or a medium-bodied red wine such as Chianti.

GRILLED RIB-EYE STEAKS WITH ROASTED GARLIC BUTTER

With Gilroy, the self-appointed Garlic Capital of the World, only an hour or two away, Bay Area residents have a special fondness for the "stinking rose." Every summer, thousands of locals flock to Gilroy for the annual garlic festival, a weekend-long extravaganza of garlic mania. A whole head of roasted garlic is a popular appetizer at casual restaurants and dinner parties. Slow roasting turns the pungent cloves creamy and mild, perfect for spreading on crisp toasts or whipping into softened butter to make a savory topping for grilled steak.

1 To make the garlic butter, preheat the oven to 325°F (165°C). Break the head of garlic into individual cloves, but do not peel them. Toss the cloves with the olive oil to coat them lightly, then wrap them loosely in an aluminum foil package. Bake the cloves until they are tender, about 40 minutes. Remove from the oven and let cool.

2 Peel the cooled cloves and cut off the hard tips. Pound them to a paste in a mortar with a pestle (or with the flat side of a chef's knife on a cutting board). Add the butter and thyme and mix until smooth. Season to taste with salt and pepper.

3 Prepare a charcoal or gas grill for direct grilling over medium-high heat.

4 Season the steaks on both sides with salt and pepper. Place the steaks on the grill rack directly over the heat and grill, turning once, to desired doneness, 4–5 minutes on each side for medium-rare.

5 Transfer the steaks to warmed individual plates. Spread an equal portion of the seasoned butter on each steak. It will melt on contact. Serve at once.

Serve with a rich, full-bodied red wine such as Cabernet Sauvignon.

FOR THE GARLIC BUTTER

1 head garlic

2 teaspoons extra-virgin olive oil

5 tablespoons (2½ oz/75 g) unsalted butter, at room temperature

2 teaspoons minced fresh thyme

Fine sea salt and freshly ground pepper

4 boneless beef rib-eye steaks, each about ¾ lb (375 g) and 1 inch (2.5 cm) thick

Fine sea salt and freshly ground pepper

Makes 4 servings

Enlightened Ranchers

Bay Area chefs and consumers are leading proponents of organic food and sustainable agriculture, a stance that local producers make possible. In times past, it would have been difficult for a chef to find a reliable source for organic meat. Today, organic chicken and beef and sustainably raised pork are available to any Bay Area cook—professional or otherwise—who seeks them out.

Launched in the late 1970s, Bay Area–based Niman Ranch has achieved the same success with naturally raised beef, pork, and lamb that Petaluma Poultry (page 145) has had with free-range and organic chicken. Founder Bill Niman started with the intention of operating a humane and ecologically sensitive livestock operation. He used natural, nonanimal feeds; allowed his animals to graze (most cattle go from weaning to feedlot) and mature slowly; and declined to use growth hormones or antibiotics on animals. Chefs found his product tastier than factory beef and more humane.

Today, other local options are available, including Prather Ranch, Marin Sun Farms, and Napa Free-Range Beef.

SLOW-ROASTED DUCK LEGS WITH CARAMELIZED TURNIPS AND TURNIP GREENS

Because of the Chinese enthusiasm for roast duck, San Franciscans who venture to Chinatown have long had access to locally raised fresh duck. Now many Bay Area markets offer these specialty birds—not only whole, but also broken down into breasts and legs. In restaurants, chefs cook the legs by the French confit method, preserving them in their own fat, and then crisping them in a pan. This recipe has the rich, slow-cooked flavor of confit but with less fat. Tender young turnips and their greens are an ideal accompaniment. Unless the turnips have lush leaves, you will need to purchase a second bunch of greens.

Fine sea salt and freshly ground black pepper

4 juniper berries

12 black peppercorns

4 duck legs, about 2 lb (1 kg) total weight

½ bunch fresh thyme

1 lb (500 g) turnip greens, thick stems removed

1 lb (500 g) turnips, thickly peeled and cut into wedges ½ inch (12 mm) wide

1 large clove garlic, minced

Pinch of red pepper flakes

Red wine vinegar

Makes 4 servings

1 Preheat the oven to 300°F (150°C). In a mortar, combine ¾ teaspoon salt, the juniper berries, and the black peppercorns and pound with a pestle until finely ground. Season the duck legs evenly with the mixture. Place a flat rack in a roasting pan. Divide the thyme sprigs into 4 equal bunches and place the bunches on the rack in 4 well-spaced mounds. Top each mound of thyme with a duck leg, skin side up.

2 Roast the duck legs for 1½ hours, then pour off and reserve the fat from the pan. Continue roasting the duck until the skin is browned and crisp, about 1 hour longer, basting once or twice with the reserved duck fat during the final hour.

3 While the duck legs are cooking, bring a large pot three-fourths full of water to a boil over high heat. Salt the boiling water, then add the turnip greens and cook just until tender, about 5 minutes. Drain in a sieve and cool quickly under running cold water. Drain again, squeeze dry, and chop coarsely.

4 About 20 minutes before the duck is ready, heat 1 tablespoon of the reserved duck fat in a frying pan over medium heat. Add the turnips, season with salt and black pepper, and toss to coat with the fat. Cook uncovered, tossing occasionally, until the turnips are tender and nicely colored, 15–20 minutes.

5 While the turnips are cooking, in another frying pan over medium-low heat, warm 1½ tablespoons of the reserved duck fat. Add the garlic and red pepper flakes and sauté briefly to release the garlic fragrance. Add the turnip greens and cook, stirring, until hot throughout. Season to taste with salt and vinegar.

6 Remove the duck from the oven and discard the thyme sprigs on the underside of each leg. Divide the duck, turnips, and turnip greens evenly among warmed individual plates, or arrange them on a large platter. Serve at once.

Serve with a medium-bodied red wine such as Pinot Noir or Merlot.

VIETNAMESE-STYLE GRILLED FIVE-SPICE CHICKEN

The many Vietnamese who settled in the San Francisco Bay Area during and after the Vietnam War introduced San Franciscans to a wealth of new dishes, ingredients, and flavors. Five-spice chicken— seasoned with Chinese five-spice powder, soy sauce, and fish sauce—became an immediate hit in the modest mom-and-pop Vietnamese restaurants that sprang up in the Richmond District and elsewhere. Look for five-spice powder in Asian markets. Manufacturers' formulas vary, but the mix always contains star anise and typically includes fennel or anise seeds, cinnamon, cloves, and Sichuan peppercorns.

1 In a small food processor, combine the garlic, shallot, ginger, and sugar and process to form a paste. Alternatively, on a cutting board, combine the ingredients and, using a large, sharp knife, mince to a paste. Transfer to a small bowl and whisk in the soy sauce, fish sauce, five-spice powder, and several grinds of pepper to make a marinade.

2 Rinse the chicken pieces in cold water and pat dry with paper towels. Place in a shallow dish and pour the marinade over the pieces. Turn the pieces in the marinade to coat. Cover and refrigerate for 8–12 hours, turning the chicken several times in the marinade. Bring to room temperature before cooking.

3 Prepare a charcoal or gas grill for direct grilling over medium heat.

4 Remove the chicken pieces from the marinade, reserving the marinade, and place skin side down on the grill rack directly over the heat. Grill on the first side until nicely browned, 11–12 minutes, basting once or twice with the marinade. Turn, baste again, and grill until the chicken juices run clear when the meat is pierced, 11–12 minutes longer. Do not baste the chicken during the final 10 minutes.

5 Remove the chicken pieces from the grill and let cool for about 5 minutes, then cut each breast in half crosswise. Transfer all the chicken pieces to a platter and serve at once.

Serve with an off-dry white wine such as Riesling or a light-bodied beer.

6 cloves garlic, sliced

1 large shallot, coarsely chopped

1 tablespoon peeled and minced fresh ginger

4 teaspoons sugar

¼ cup (2 fl oz/60 ml) soy sauce

¼ cup (2 fl oz/60 ml) Thai or Vietnamese fish sauce

½ teaspoon five-spice powder (page 186)

Freshly ground pepper

1 chicken, about 3 lb (1.5 kg), cut into 8 serving pieces (2 wings, 2 legs, 2 thighs, 2 breasts), plus 2 additional wings

Makes 4 servings

SEARED AHI TUNA WITH WARM WHITE BEAN SALAD

Many Bay Area diners first encounter ahi tuna in sushi bars, then discover that it is just as delicious cooked as raw. Some cooks like to sear it briefly so it is still rare in the center; others prefer it more fully cooked. Be wary of cooking this fish too long, or it will be dry. You can cook the beans a day ahead, refrigerate them in their cooking liquid, then reheat them and make the salad just before cooking the tuna. In Italy, a salad of canned tuna and white beans, served at room temperature, is a popular antipasto. Similarly, you can cool the tuna in this recipe after searing it, then flake it into the prepared beans.

FOR COOKING THE BEANS

1 cup (7 oz/220 g) dried cannellini beans

1 carrot, peeled and cut into 4 or 5 chunks

1 celery stalk, cut into 4 or 5 chunks

½ yellow onion

1 clove garlic, lightly smashed

Fine sea salt

FOR THE BEAN SALAD

1 large tomato, cored, peeled, seeded (page 187), and diced

½ small red onion, minced

1 large clove garlic, finely minced

2 tablespoons chopped fresh basil

1 tablespoon chopped fresh flat-leaf (Italian) parsley

3 tablespoons extra-virgin olive oil

2 teaspoons red wine vinegar, or to taste

Sea salt and freshly ground pepper

1 teaspoon fennel seeds

4 ahi tuna steaks, each about 6 oz (185 g)

2 tablespoons extra-virgin olive oil

Makes 4 servings

1 To cook the beans, pick them over, discarding any misshapen beans and grit. Rinse well, place in a bowl with water to cover generously, and let soak overnight. Drain the beans, put in a saucepan, and add the carrot, celery, onion, garlic, and water to cover by 1 inch (2.5 cm). Place over medium-low heat and bring to a simmer slowly. Cover and adjust the heat to maintain a bare simmer. Cook until the beans are tender, about 45 minutes or longer, depending on their age. Remove from the heat, season to taste with salt, and let cool in the liquid until just warm. Remove and discard the carrot, celery, onion, and garlic.

2 To make the bean salad, drain the warm beans, reserving the liquid for soup. Put the beans in a bowl and add the tomato, red onion, garlic, basil, parsley, olive oil, and vinegar. Stir gently, then season to taste with salt and pepper.

3 To prepare the tuna, using a mortar and pestle or a spice grinder, finely grind the fennel seeds. Rub the tuna steaks on both sides with 1 tablespoon of the olive oil. Season on both sides with salt, pepper, and fennel seeds.

4 Choose a heavy frying pan large enough to hold all the tuna steaks in a single layer without touching, or use 2 smaller frying pans. Place over high heat until hot, then add the remaining 1 tablespoon olive oil and swirl to coat the bottom. When the oil is hot, add the tuna steaks, reduce the heat to medium, and cook until nicely colored on the bottom and cooked about halfway through, 1 minute or longer, depending on thickness. Turn and cook until the steaks are moist and pink, not red, in the center, about 1 minute longer.

5 Divide the tuna among warmed individual plates. Surround with the warm bean salad, dividing it evenly. Serve at once.

Serve with a dry rosé.

BRAISED CHICKEN WITH TOMATO, PANCETTA, AND ZINFANDEL

Bay Area wine drinkers are such fans of Zinfandel that they turn out by the thousands for the ZAP (Zinfandel Advocates and Producers) tasting held in San Francisco each winter. With its reputation as a wine for relaxed occasions, Zinfandel complements winter stews and braises, especially when tomato sauce is involved. For this dish, many Bay Area cooks would use a bird from Sonoma County's Petaluma Poultry—either the free-range Rocky or his sibling Rosie, the nation's first certified organic chicken. Serve this dish with creamy polenta.

1 Strain the mushroom liquid through dampened cheesecloth (muslin) into a bowl. Set aside.

2 Rinse the chicken pieces, pat dry with paper towels, and season with salt and pepper.

3 Place a large frying pan over medium-high until hot. Add the olive oil and swirl to coat the bottom. When the oil is almost smoking, add the chicken in one layer, skin side down. Reduce the heat to medium and cook until browned, about 8 minutes, then turn and brown on the other side, about 8 minutes longer. Transfer to a platter and pour off all but 1 tablespoon fat.

4 Return the pan to medium-low heat and add the pancetta. Cook, stirring, until the pancetta crisps, about 1 minute. Add the garlic and sage and cook, stirring, for about 1 minute. Add the wine and simmer briefly, scraping the browned bits from the pan bottom with a wooden spoon. Add the tomatoes and the porcini and their liquid. Bring to a simmer, adjust the heat to maintain a gentle simmer, and cook, uncovered, for 15 minutes. Add a little water if the sauce is too dry.

5 Preheat the oven to 200°F (95°C). Return the chicken to the pan, cover, and simmer gently, turning it once in the sauce, until tender, 15 minutes. As the pieces are done, transfer them to a heatproof serving platter kept in the oven. (The breasts may be done first.) If the sauce seems thin, raise the heat to high and simmer until thickened. Spoon the sauce over the chicken and garnish with the parsley. Serve at once.

Serve with a spicy red wine such as Zinfandel.

½ oz (15 g) dried porcini (ceps) mushrooms, soaked in ¾ cup (6 fl oz/180 ml) hot water until softened, drained, reserving liquid, and chopped

1 chicken, about 3½ lb (1.75 g), cut into 8 serving pieces (2 wings, 2 legs, 2 thighs, 2 breasts)

Fine sea salt and freshly ground pepper

1 tablespoon extra-virgin olive oil

3 oz (90 g) pancetta, minced

2 large cloves garlic, minced

1 tablespoon minced fresh sage

½ cup (4 fl oz/125 ml) Zinfandel

1 can (14½ oz/455 g) plum (Roma) tomatoes with juice, puréed in a blender

1½ tablespoons minced fresh flat-leaf (Italian) parsley

Makes 4 servings

Meat Takes the Cure

Whether they need pancetta, prosciutto, or pâté, Bay Area cooks can buy a product made locally. The traditions of the French charcuterie and Italian *salumeria* thrive in several Bay Area businesses devoted to the craft of cured meats and sausage.

P. G. Molinari was a Piedmontese immigrant who established a salami factory in North Beach in 1896 and opened a deli a decade later. Today, locals needing *soppressata* or mortadella know they can still find Molinari products at the original deli and in markets all over town.

French food enthusiasts have looked to local charcuterie producer Marcel et Henri for pâtés, galantines, and duck liver mousse since the 1960s. In the 1980s, retired economist Hobbs Shore found a second career when chefs began clamoring for the meats he smoked as a hobby. Today, his applewood-smoked bacon, prosciutto, and pancetta are favorites. Another local business, Aidells Sausage Company, revolutionized the sausage world by introducing fresh, contemporary flavors such as sun-dried tomatoes and chicken-apple.

SIDE DISHES

All the best Northern California produce flows to San Francisco

markets, enticing cooks to put seasonal vegetables front and center.

Perhaps because they live so close to the source, Bay Area diners have a passion for vegetables. Compared to cooks elsewhere, they are undeniably lucky, accustomed to working with produce less than forty-eight hours out of the ground. With such quality at their fingertips, locals have learned to prepare vegetables simply, often presenting them with little more than a well-chosen seasoning. They might use a pinch of crushed aniseeds to heighten the flavor of roasted beets, chipotle chiles to enliven sweet corn, a spoonful of Thai chile paste to punch up a long bean stir-fry, or a drizzle of local olive oil on creamy, roasted fingerling potatoes.

GARLIC-AND-ROSEMARY-ROASTED FINGERLING POTATOES

First introduced at Bay Area farmers' markets by growers aiming at the gourmet niche, fingerling potatoes—so called because of their slender, elongated shape—have found a broad audience. They are thin-skinned, dense, and waxy, and they cook quickly because they're small. Roasted in a stainless-steel pan at high heat with fresh herbs and garlic, they will brown beautifully and perfume the kitchen as they cook. The smaller garlic cloves alongside the potatoes will probably be too caramelized to eat, but larger cloves should be soft and creamy.

1 Preheat the oven to 425°F (220°C). In a large bowl, toss the potatoes with the olive oil until evenly coated. Transfer to a stainless-steel roasting pan or frying pan large enough to accommodate them in a single layer. Season with salt.

2 Break the head of garlic into individual cloves, but do not peel them. Scatter the garlic cloves around the potatoes. Pull the rosemary leaves off the stem and scatter them around the potatoes as well.

3 Bake the potatoes, stirring once or twice, until they are nicely browned and the tip of a knife pierces them easily, about 30 minutes. Transfer to a warmed bowl and serve at once.

1½ lb (750 g) fingerling potatoes or other waxy potatoes

2 tablespoons extra-virgin olive oil

Fine sea salt

1 head garlic

1 fresh rosemary sprig, about 6 inches (15 cm) long

Makes 4 servings

Liquid Gold

Like the winemakers who are often their neighbors, a new generation of Northern California olive growers is determined to make a product as fine as any in Europe. Alongside the imported oils in Bay Area markets, shoppers will find handsomely packaged oils from local producers.

Because olives and grapes tend to thrive in similar soils and environments, many of the new oil producers are in fact wineries. Some, such as Long Meadow Ranch in St. Helena, are working with trees that have been on the property for decades. Others, such as Araujo, have imported trees from France and Italy, selecting varieties renowned for quality.

Two Bay Area producers determined to make extra-virgin olive oil a viable business are DaVero in Healdsburg and McEvoy Ranch in Petaluma. Both use exclusively Tuscan olive varieties to produce highly aromatic oils with the piquancy of their Tuscan counterparts.

To maintain high standards, producers have formed the California Olive Oil Council. To earn its "Certified Extra Virgin" seal denoting quality, the oil must pass a rigorous tasting panel.

SOFT POLENTA WITH TELEME CHEESE

Long before polenta became fashionable in Italianate restaurants coast to coast, San Franciscans could buy the coarse cornmeal readily in North Beach. Today, a side dish of polenta is almost as familiar to Bay Area diners as mashed potatoes and is widely seen on menus as an accompaniment to braised short ribs, lamb shanks, or pork roast. The secret to great polenta is to cook it the full forty-five minutes, until it is no longer grainy. Poured out onto a platter or wooden board, it makes a rustic family-style side dish. Peluso Cheese Company in Los Banos is not the only producer of California Teleme, but it is widely considered the best.

4 tablespoons (2 oz/60 g) unsalted butter

½ large yellow onion, finely minced

1 bay leaf

1 cup (5 oz/155 g) polenta

¼ cup (1 oz/30 g) grated Parmesan cheese

Fine sea salt and freshly ground pepper

¼ lb (125 g) Teleme cheese, preferably Peluso brand (page 68), at room temperature

Makes 6 servings

1 In a large saucepan over medium-low heat, melt 2 tablespoons of the butter. Add the onion and sauté until softened, about 10 minutes.

2 Meanwhile, bring 5 cups (40 fl oz/1.25 l) water to a boil. Add the boiling water and the bay leaf to the onion mixture and bring to a simmer.

3 Gradually add the polenta to the simmering water while whisking constantly. When the mixture begins to thicken, switch to a wooden spoon. Adjust the heat so the mixture bubbles slowly but steadily. Cook, stirring often, until the polenta is smooth and no longer gritty, about 45 minutes, thinning with more boiling water if it gets too thick before it is ready. Taste often, and remove the bay leaf when it has imparted enough flavor. Stir in the Parmesan and the remaining 2 tablespoons butter, season to taste with salt, and remove from the heat.

4 Pour the polenta onto a large platter or wooden cutting board. Cut the Teleme into 10 or 12 slivers and arrange them on top, tucking them into the polenta slightly so they melt in its heat. Grind some pepper over the polenta and serve at once.

ROASTED BEETS WITH ANISE

Beets may be red in most of the country, but in San Francisco, they come in a rainbow of hues. Pink, golden, pink-and-white bull's eye, and even white beets tempt cooks to make this humble vegetable a side-dish star. A sherry vinaigrette with crushed aniseeds complements beets of any color. Pair them with roast pork, pork chops, or duck. If you want to mix beets of different colors, roast and dress the red beets separately, as they will stain the others. The best, sweetest beets will still have perky greens attached, a sign of freshness. Don't throw away the greens. Boil them briefly, squeeze them dry, and reheat with olive oil and garlic.

1 Preheat the oven to 400°F (200°C). If the beet greens are still attached, cut them off, leaving 1 inch (2.5 cm) of the stem intact to avoid piercing the skin (leave the root attached as well). Save the greens for another use. Put the beets in a baking dish with water to a depth of ¼ inch (6 mm). Cover and bake until the beets are easily pierced with the tip of a knife, about 1 hour.

2 Remove the beets from the oven and, when cool enough to handle, peel the beets and trim the roots. Cut the beets into wedges, place them in a bowl, and toss them with the vinegar while they are still warm.

3 Using a mortar and pestle or a spice grinder, finely grind the aniseeds. In a small bowl, whisk together the olive oil, garlic, and ground aniseeds. Pour the mixture over the warm beets and toss well to coat evenly. Season to taste with salt. Serve the beets warm, at room temperature, or chilled.

6 beets, about 1½ lb (750 g) total weight without greens

1½ tablespoons sherry vinegar

Scant 1 teaspoon aniseeds

2 tablespoons extra-virgin olive oil

1 small clove garlic, finely minced

Fine sea salt

Makes 4 servings

STIR-FRIED LONG BEANS WITH THAI CHILE PASTE

Chinese long beans, also known as yard-long beans, can be eighteen inches (45 cm) or more in length. Most are dark green, but a pale green variety also turns up in Asian markets. Bay Area supermarkets regularly stock long beans, a sign of their popularity among non-Asians who appreciate their full flavor and chewy texture. In Chinese restaurants, they are often stir-fried with ground pork and seasonings such as garlic and ginger. Here they are stir-fried with Thai roasted chile paste, fish sauce, and aromatic Thai basil, which has a more licorice-like perfume than Mediterranean basil. Serve with roast chicken and rice.

Fine sea salt

1 lb (500 g) Chinese long beans, ends trimmed and cut into 4-inch (10-cm) lengths

1½ tablespoons peanut oil

1½ tablespoons Thai roasted chile paste (page 187)

1 tablespoon Thai or Vietnamese fish sauce (page 186)

⅓ cup (⅓ oz/10 g) fresh Thai basil leaves

Makes 4 servings

1 Bring a large pot of water to a boil over high heat. Salt the boiling water, then add the long beans and cook until barely tender, about 3 minutes. Drain in a sieve and rinse with cold running water to stop the cooking. Thoroughly pat dry.

2 Place a wok or large frying pan over medium-high heat and heat until hot. Add the peanut oil and swirl to coat the bottom. Add the long beans and the chile paste and stir-fry until the beans are evenly coated with the seasoning. The chile paste will clump at first but will eventually dissolve and coat the beans nicely. If the beans are still a little underdone, add a tablespoon or two of water, cover, and let them steam until they are done to your taste. Uncover and sprinkle with the fish sauce.

3 Remove from the heat, add the basil, and toss to distribute the leaves evenly. Transfer to a warmed serving dish and serve at once.

GORDON'S RED POTATO SALAD WITH WHOLE-GRAIN MUSTARD DRESSING

Napa Valley vintners travel the world promoting their wine in fancy restaurants, but when they're at home, many have a soft spot for Gordon's. This modest café and wine bar is arguably the heart of the Yountville community. On Sunday mornings, locals ritually head here for coffee and eggs as if it were their own breakfast room. And at lunchtime, owners Sally Gordon and Mari Jennings accompany their generous sandwiches with a mustardy potato salad that is locally famous. Serve with corned-beef sandwiches or alongside grilled sausages.

1 In a large pot, combine the potatoes with water to cover by 1 inch (2.5 cm). Salt the water, place over high heat, and bring to a boil. Reduce the heat to medium and simmer gently, uncovered, until the potatoes are just tender when pierced with the tip of a knife, about 10 minutes. Test the potatoes often and be careful not to overcook them.

2 While the potatoes are cooking, in a large bowl, combine the mayonnaise, parsley, tarragon, capers, onion, whole-grain and Dijon mustards, ½ teaspoon salt, and 2 tablespoons water. Whisk to blend, then season to taste with pepper.

3 Drain the potatoes and immediately add them to the dressing. Toss well to coat evenly, then let cool to room temperature. Cover and refrigerate until chilled. Thin the dressing at serving time with a little more water if needed.

2 lb (1 kg) small, round red-skinned potatoes, quartered

Fine sea salt and freshly ground pepper

½ cup (4 fl oz/125 ml) homemade or store-bought mayonnaise

½ cup (¾ oz/20 g) chopped fresh flat-leaf (Italian) parsley

1½ tablespoons chopped fresh tarragon

2 tablespoons chopped capers

¼ large red onion, thinly sliced

1 tablespoon whole-grain mustard

1½ teaspoons Dijon mustard

Makes 6 servings

Wine Country Dining

For many years, the dining-out scene in Napa Valley lagged behind the reputation of its wines. Locals sometimes joked that the best restaurant in Napa was a steakhouse in Sonoma.

No longer. Today, visitors are drawn to the Napa Valley not only for the famed wines but also for the equally praiseworthy food. Certainly the ultimate in reverse chic is Taylor's Refresher, an updated St. Helena burger joint with self-service and outdoor seating. Diners looking for a slightly more formal experience would probably head to Napa's Bistro Don Giovanni, an outpost of Cal-Ital cooking, or to one of Yountville's two ultra-French bistros, Bouchon and Bistro Jeanty.

Napa Valley residents are understandably proud of the famed French Laundry, a Yountville restaurant with worldwide acclaim, but the valley's less haute dining rooms offer no end of pleasure.

Neighboring Sonoma County also offers many dining options. For lunch, Taqueria El Sombrero in Sonoma makes truly exceptional tacos. For a relaxed dinner accompanied by local wines, stylish Dry Creek Kitchen is a Healdsburg favorite.

GIANT WHITE BEANS WITH SAGE AND TOMATO

The Greek gigandes *beans grown by Phipps Ranch in Pescadero are a Bay Area favorite, admired for their impressive size, meatiness, and creamy texture. They are off-white, elongated, and astoundingly plump. In Greece, they often appear cooked with tomato, as here, or with roasted red peppers (capsicums). They make a fine partner for roast lamb, pan-seared pork chops, or grilled sausages. Like most dried-bean dishes, this one is even better made a day ahead. You can purchase* gigandes *from Phipps Ranch (see page 187).*

1 To cook the beans, rinse them well, place in a bowl with water to cover generously, and let them soak overnight. Drain the beans, put in a large saucepan, and add the carrot, celery, onion, garlic, bay leaf, and water to cover by 1 inch (2.5 cm). Place over medium-low heat and bring to a simmer slowly. Cover and adjust the heat to maintain a bare simmer. Cook until the beans are tender, about 1 hour or longer, depending on their age. Remove from the heat and let cool in the liquid. Remove and discard the carrot, celery, onion, garlic, and bay leaf. Drain the beans, reserving the liquid. Set aside.

2 In a large frying pan over medium-low heat, warm the ¼ cup olive oil. Add the onion, garlic, sage, and red pepper flakes and sauté until the onion is softened, about 10 minutes. Add the tomato and oregano, crushing the herb between your fingers. Bring to a simmer and cook, stirring occasionally, for about 5 minutes to blend the flavors. Add a little of the bean liquid if the mixture threatens to become dry.

3 Add the beans and enough of their cooking liquid to cover them barely. Season with salt and bring to a simmer. Cover partially and simmer gently until the beans have absorbed most of the liquid, about 30 minutes. Remove from the heat and let the beans stand for 15 minutes before serving.

4 Just before serving, stir in a little additional olive oil for flavor, then divide the beans among warmed individual plates. Serve at once.

FOR COOKING THE BEANS

1½ cups (10½ oz/330 g) dried *gigandes* beans or other large dried white beans such as cannellini

1 carrot, cut into 5 or 6 chunks

1 celery stalk, cut into 5 or 6 chunks

½ yellow onion

2 cloves garlic, lightly smashed

1 bay leaf

¼ cup (2 fl oz/60 ml) extra-virgin olive oil, plus more for finishing

½ large yellow onion, minced

2 cloves garlic, minced

1 tablespoon chopped fresh sage

Generous pinch of red pepper flakes

¾ cup (4½ oz/140 g) finely chopped canned tomato with some juice

½ teaspoon dried oregano

Fine sea salt

Makes 6 servings

Farming on the Urban Edge

With the climate all but guaranteeing a year-round growing season, the greater Bay Area could be an agricultural paradise. And in times past, it was. Sadly, urbanization has caused most farms near the city to fold. Those that remain are treasured by residents.

South of San Francisco, Iacopi Farm in Half Moon Bay is one surviving member of a once-thriving Italian farming community. The farm's fava (broad) beans, peas, romano beans, and cranberry beans are favorites at local markets. Nearby, in Pescadero, Phipps Ranch harvests shell beans that sell briskly.

In Brentwood, east of San Francisco, Rick and Kristie Knoll have built a successful small farm specializing in figs, green garlic, fava beans, and stone fruits. Neighboring Frog Hollow Farm is renowned for its tree-ripened peaches and juicy white nectarines, and for delicious jams and pastries.

Just north of San Francisco, Green Gulch Farm grows impeccable salad greens and beets, while Star Route Farm has built its reputation on greens and offbeat produce like nettles and purslane.

CORN ON THE COB WITH CHIPOTLE-LIME BUTTER

Little known outside the Mexican community until the 1990s, chipotle chiles have been a huge crossover hit. Bay Area cooks like their smoky flavor (a chipotle is a dried and smoked jalapeño) and improvise with them freely, adding them to soups, sauces, and stews. Canned chipotles in adobo sauce—whole chiles preserved with tomato, vinegar, and spices—can be found in Mexican markets and most supermarkets. Paired with butter and lime, the chiles give midsummer's corn on the cob zesty spice and would be equally welcome slathered on hot grilled shrimp (prawns). Store leftover chipotles in the refrigerator in an airtight glass jar.

FOR THE BUTTER

½ cup (4 oz/125 g) unsalted butter, at room temperature

3 tablespoons minced fresh cilantro (fresh coriander)

1 tablespoon grated lime zest

1 chipotle chile in adobo sauce, finely minced

Fine sea salt

6 large ears corn, yellow or white, husked

Makes 6 servings

1 To make the butter, combine the butter, cilantro, lime zest, and chipotle chile and mix with a spoon until smooth. Season to taste with salt.

2 Bring a large pot three-fourths full of water to a boil over high heat. Add the corn, cover, and remove from the heat. Let stand for 5 minutes.

3 Using tongs, lift the ears of corn from the boiling water onto a kitchen towel to drain briefly, then transfer to a serving platter or individual plates. Slather with the seasoned butter, dividing it evenly. You may not need it all. Serve at once.

DESSERTS

Many Bay Area dessert fans lean toward sweets that celebrate

the harvest, but most agree that chocolate is always in season.

As much as any other part of the meal, Bay Area desserts acknowledge the seasons, often incorporating the fruits of the moment. Most local cooks have little interest in fruits from the Southern Hemisphere because the Bay Area's winter market has its own lures, such as citrus, pomegranates, and nuts. Fragrant Meyer lemons scent ice creams, cakes, and *pots de crème* in winter. In spring, plump strawberries turn up in luscious shortcakes and sundaes. Summer's fruit bonanza inspires colorful galettes, and autumn offers a wealth of pears, persimmons, and apples. And year-round, Bay Area diners prove their affection for chocolate in any form.

STRAWBERRY SUNDAE WITH MASCARPONE ICE CREAM

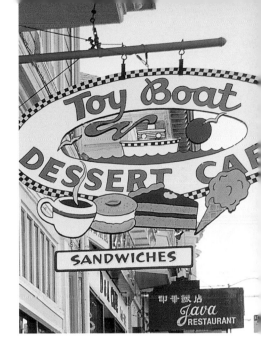

You don't have to be a child to succumb to the lure of a sundae, especially one made with strawberries and mascarpone ice cream. Serve it in a clear parfait glass so you can see the layers of bright red berry sauce, sliced berries, and melting ice cream. Mascarpone resembles French crème fraîche, although it is thicker and not as tangy. It is made with coagulated cream drained until it is as spreadable as cake frosting. Used in ice cream, mascarpone contributes a flavor reminiscent of cheesecake. Fresh strawberries are the ideal companion, especially the fragrant summer berries from Watsonville, south of San Francisco.

1 To make the ice cream, in a saucepan, combine the half-and-half and cream. Using the tip of a knife, scrape the vanilla seeds from the pod halves into the cream, whisk to blend, then add the pod halves. Place over medium-low heat, bring to a simmer, cover, remove from the heat, and let steep for 15 minutes.

2 In a bowl, whisk together the egg yolks and sugar until the mixture is pale yellow and forms a ribbon when the whisk is lifted. This should take about 3 minutes. Gradually whisk in the hot cream mixture (including the vanilla pod). Return the mixture to the saucepan and cook over medium-low heat, stirring constantly with a wooden spoon, until the mixture visibly thickens and coats the spoon. (It should reach 178°F/81°C on an instant-read thermometer.) Do not let it boil, or it will curdle.

3 Immediately remove the custard from the heat and stir for 1 minute. Let cool for 15 minutes, then whisk in the mascarpone. Pour through a medium-mesh sieve into a bowl. Cover and refrigerate until well chilled, about 6 hours or overnight.

4 Freeze in an ice-cream maker according to the manufacturer's directions. Transfer to an airtight container and place in the freezer.

5 To make the sauce, in a nonreactive saucepan, stir together the strawberries, sugar, and lemon juice. Let stand for 1 hour, stirring once or twice to dissolve the sugar. Place the pan over medium heat, bring to a simmer, and simmer gently for 5 minutes. Remove from the heat, let cool, cover, and refrigerate until well chilled, about 6 hours.

6 Just before serving, toast the almonds: Preheat the oven to 325°F (165°C). Spread the almonds on a baking sheet and toast until lightly colored and fragrant, about 10 minutes. Let cool.

7 To assemble the sundaes, put a scoop of ice cream in each parfait glass. Top with a few sliced strawberries and 2 tablespoons of the strawberry sauce. Add a second scoop of ice cream, more strawberries, and another 2 tablespoons of sauce to each glass. Top with the almonds, dividing them evenly. Serve at once.

FOR THE ICE CREAM

1 cup (8 fl oz/250 ml) half-and-half (half cream)

1 cup (8 fl oz/250 ml) heavy (double) cream

½ vanilla bean, split lengthwise

6 large egg yolks

⅔ cup (5 oz/155 g) sugar

1 cup (8 oz/250 g) mascarpone

FOR THE SAUCE

2 cups (8 oz/250 g) strawberries, stems removed and coarsely chopped

7 tablespoons (3½ oz/105 g) sugar

1 teaspoon fresh lemon juice

½ cup (2 oz/60 g) sliced (flaked) almonds

2 cups (8 oz/250 g) strawberries, stems removed and sliced

Makes 6 servings

PLUM AND BLACKBERRY SORBET

The addition of blackberries gives this sorbet a magnificent deep-plum color and a more complex flavor than you could obtain from plums alone. Accompany it with buttery nut cookies or biscotti. If you make the sorbet several hours ahead, remove it from the freezer and let it soften for a few minutes so that it is easier to scoop. You can use any fragrant, flavorful plum in this recipe; the blackberries or olallieberries (a plump, juicy blackberry hybrid) will contribute plenty of color even if the plums are pale-fleshed. The dark-skinned, amber-fleshed Santa Rosa plum, widely planted in Northern California, would be the local favorite.

⅔ cup (5 oz/155 g) sugar

⅔ cup (5 fl oz/160 ml) water

1 lb (500 g) plums, pitted

1½ cups (6 oz/185 g) blackberries or olallieberries, plus more for serving

Makes 4 servings

1 In a small saucepan over medium heat, combine the sugar and water. Bring to a boil, stirring to dissolve the sugar. Remove from the heat and let the mixture cool completely.

2 In a food processor, combine the plums and black-berries and process until a smooth purée forms. Pass the purée through a fine-mesh sieve placed over a bowl, pressing firmly on the solids with a rubber spatula to push as much of the purée through the sieve as possible while leaving the seeds and skins behind. Stir in the cooled sugar syrup. Cover and refrigerate until well chilled, about 6 hours or overnight.

3 Freeze the sorbet base in an ice-cream maker according to the manufacturer's directions. Transfer to an airtight container and place in the freezer. Serve with a few berries scattered on top.

BUTTERMILK PANNA COTTA WITH SUMMER FRUIT COMPOTE

A soft and quivery panna cotta *with the subtle tang of buttermilk makes a lovely partner for mixed summer fruits. In northern Italy, where the dessert orginates,* panna cotta *(literally, cooked cream) would be made entirely with heavy cream. Adding buttermilk lightens the dessert and contributes the intriguing, pleasantly tart taste of a cultured dairy product. This dessert makes use of the extraordinary bounty of summer berries, figs, and stone fruits that are available in San Francisco farmer's markets.*

1 To make the *panna cotta*, moisten a paper towel with the oil and very lightly oil six ¾-cup (6–fl oz/180-ml) ramekins or custard cups.

2 Put the water in a small, heatproof ramekin. Sprinkle the gelatin evenly over the water and let stand to soften for 10 minutes. Set the ramekin in a small saucepan, and add water to the pan to come halfway up the side of the ramekin. Place over medium heat and bring the water just to a simmer to dissolve the gelatin. Set the saucepan aside with the ramekin in it.

3 In another small saucepan over medium heat, combine the cream and granulated sugar and bring to a simmer, stirring constantly. Remove from the heat, then whisk in the gelatin. Let cool for 1 minute, then whisk in the buttermilk and the almond extract. Divide the mixture evenly among the prepared molds. Cover and refrigerate until firm, at least 4 hours or overnight.

4 To make the compote, in a large bowl, combine the fruits, superfine sugar, lemon juice, and liqueur. Stir gently to distribute evenly, cover, and refrigerate for 4–8 hours, stirring occasionally.

5 To unmold each *panna cotta*, place the ramekin in a bowl of hot water for about 10 seconds. Then invert a dessert plate on top of the ramekin and invert the ramekin and plate together. Shake the mold gently to loosen the *panna cotta*; it should slip out easily. Surround each *panna cotta* with the fruit compote, dividing it evenly. Serve at once.

Serve with a rich, golden late-harvest Riesling.

FOR THE PANNA COTTA

Canola or vegetable oil for oiling the molds

2 tablespoons water

1½ teaspoons unflavored gelatin

2 cups (16 fl oz/500 ml) heavy (double) cream

7 tablespoons (3½ oz/105 g) granulated sugar

1 cup (8 fl oz/250 ml) buttermilk

⅛ teaspoon almond extract (essence)

FOR THE COMPOTE

4 cups (1¼–1½ lb/625–750 g) mixed summer fruits such as pitted and sliced plums, nectarines, peeled peaches, figs, and whole berries

2 tablespoons superfine (caster) sugar, or to taste

2½ teaspoons fresh lemon juice, or to taste

2 teaspoons anise liqueur such as sambuca, or to taste

Makes 6 servings

Dessert Wines

With a wedge of blue cheese or a delicate *panna cotta,* no wine works as well as a sweet wine. Unfortunately, high-quality dessert wines are exceedingly expensive to make, and only a handful of Northern California wineries attempt them.

Dolce in Napa Valley is the only North American winery devoted exclusively to a single dessert wine, as, for example, Château d'Yquem is in France. Introduced with the 1989 vintage and made from Sémillon and Sauvignon Blanc grapes, Dolce rivals its French counterparts.

One of the most acclaimed Northern California dessert wines, Beringer Vineyards' Nightingale has its own unique history. Like Sauternes, it is made with Sémillon and Sauvignon Blanc grapes. But in the early 1980s, winemaker Myron Nightingale, working with his wife Alice, realized that he didn't have to depend on nature to create the conditions demanded by botrytis, the "noble rot" that attacks grapes and concentrates their sugar. Alice devised a method for culturing botrytis, allowing Beringer to create artificially what nature—in good years—does naturally. Thus, Nightingale can be made every year.

MUSCAT-POACHED PEARS AND DRIED CHERRIES WITH MUSCAT SABAYON

In California, Muscat wines are made in a range of styles. Some are barely sweet and delightful as a chilled aperitif. Others are considerably sweeter and intended for dessert. You may need to adjust the sugar in the pear poaching liquid accordingly. This recipe was developed with a Muscat of medium sweetness. If you can't find a Muscat, you can poach the pears with an off-dry white wine, although the poaching liquid will not be quite as flavorful. You can use dried sweet or sour (pie) cherries, but if possible, purchase cherries that have not been additionally sweetened. Farmers' markets and natural-food stores are good sources.

1¼ cups (10 fl oz/310 ml)
California Muscat wine

1¼ cups (10 fl oz/310 ml) water

½ cup (4 oz/125 g) sugar,
or to taste

2 wide lemon zest strips

3 firm yet ripe large pears such as
Bosc or Bartlett (Williams'), peeled,
halved, and cored

½ cup (3 oz/90 g) dried cherries

FOR THE SABAYON

½ cup (4 fl oz/125 ml) heavy
(double) cream

4 large egg yolks

3 tablespoons sugar

½ cup (4 fl oz/125 ml) California
Muscat wine

Makes 6 servings

1 In a wide saucepan just large enough to hold the pear halves, combine the wine, water, sugar, and lemon zest. Place over medium heat and bring to a simmer, stirring until the sugar dissolves.

2 Add the pear halves, cover with a round piece of parchment (baking) paper, and adjust the heat to maintain a gentle simmer. Cook, uncovered, until the pears are perhaps half-done, about 10 minutes, depending on their size and firmness. Carefully turn them over, add the cherries, replace the parchment, and continue cooking at a gentle simmer until the tip of a knife just pierces the pears easily, about 10 minutes longer.

3 Using a slotted spoon, transfer the pears and cherries to a bowl. Remove and discard the lemon zest, then return the poaching liquid to high heat and simmer until it is reduced to 1 cup (8 fl oz/250 ml). Remove from the heat and let cool to room temperature. Pour the liquid over the pears and cherries, cover, and refrigerate until well chilled, about 6 hours.

4 When you are ready to serve the pears, make the sabayon: In a bowl, use a whisk or a handheld mixer at medium speed to beat the cream to firm peaks. Cover and refrigerate until needed.

5 Have ready a large bowl half full of ice water. In the top pan of a double boiler or in a heatproof bowl, whisk together the egg yolks and sugar until pale yellow. Set over (not touching) barely simmering water in the lower pan or a saucepan and continue whisking until the mixture lightens and thickens and the whisk leaves a trail, 2–3 minutes. Gradually whisk in the wine and continue whisking until the mixture is pale, thick, fluffy, and greatly expanded in volume, about 10 minutes. Do not overcook or you may scramble the eggs. If the sabayon is cooking too fast, lift the pan or bowl from over the water for a minute or two as you whisk.

6 Remove the pan or bowl from over the water and place it in the ice water to chill quickly. Whisk occasionally to help speed the cooling. When it is cool, gently fold in the whipped cream.

7 Using a slotted spoon, transfer the pear halves, cut side up, to individual dessert plates. For a more elegant presentation, set the pears cut side down on a cutting board. Starting from the blossom end, thinly slice each half lengthwise, leaving the slices attached at the stem end. Transfer each pear half to a dessert plate. Gently press on the pears to fan the slices.

8 Spoon some of the cherries and a little of the syrup over each pear half. Accompany with a large spoonful of sabayon.

Serve with a sweet California Muscat.

STEAMED PERSIMMON PUDDING WITH BRANDIED WHIPPED CREAM

Visitors to California who have never seen ripe persimmons on a tree are often astonished by the sight. By the time the fruits ripen to a deep pumpkin-orange, the trees have dropped their leaves, leaving the late-autumn crop dangling like Christmas ornaments. The trees bear profusely, and much of the fruit ends up in spicy steamed puddings such as this one. Note that you will need a two-quart (2-l) pudding mold with a lid, preferably one that clamps in place. You will also need a pot deep enough to hold the mold, set on a rack, with enough head space to cover the pot. If you have a pasta insert, you can set the mold in that.

1 Using a pastry brush, coat the bottom and sides of a 2-qt (2-l) lidded pudding mold (see Note) with melted butter. Sprinkle the bottom and sides of the mold with sugar, then tap out the excess.

2 Halve the persimmons and discard the stems. Remove the seeds, if any. Scoop out the pulp with a table spoon and discard the skin. In a food processor or blender, purée the pulp until smooth. Measure out 2 cups (18 oz/560 g) purée and set aside.

3 Preheat the oven to 350°F (180°C). Spread the walnuts on a baking sheet and toast until fragrant and lightly browned, about 10 minutes. Pour onto a plate, let cool, and then chop. Set aside.

4 In a bowl, stir together the flour, baking soda, cinnamon, ginger, nutmeg, salt, and cloves.

5 In a large bowl, using a wooden spoon, beat together the sugar, melted butter, brandy, lemon juice, vanilla, and eggs. Beat in the persimmon pulp until incorporated, then stir in the raisins and walnuts. Add the dry ingredients, stirring until well blended. Pour into the prepared mold and cover it.

6 Set the mold on a rack in a large pot. Add boiling water to come halfway up the sides of the mold. Cover the pot, place over medium heat, and bring to a gentle simmer, adjusting the heat as necessary. Cook for 2 hours, checking occasionally and adding boiling water as needed to keep the water level constant.

7 Remove the mold from the pot. Remove the lid, and let the pudding cool in the mold on a rack until just warm, about 1½ hours. Invert onto a serving platter.

8 At serving time, make the whipped cream. In a large bowl, using a whisk or handheld mixer, whip the cream until soft peaks form. Add sugar and brandy to taste and beat just until combined.

9 Slice the warm pudding and accompany each slice with a dollop of whipped cream.

Serve with a late-harvest dessert wine such as Gewürztraminer or a sweet sherry.

1¾ lb (875 g) very ripe Hachiya persimmons

⅔ cup *each* walnuts (3½ oz/105 g) and raisins (4 oz/125 g)

1⅔ cups (8½ oz/265 g) unbleached all-purpose (plain) flour

1 tablespoon baking soda (bicarbonate of soda)

½ teaspoon *each* ground cinnamon and ground ginger

¼ teaspoon *each* freshly grated nutmeg and fine sea salt

⅛ teaspoon ground cloves

1¼ cups (10 oz/315 g) sugar

½ cup (4 oz/125 g) unsalted butter, melted

2½ tablespoons brandy

1 tablespoon fresh lemon juice

2 teaspoons vanilla extract (essence)

3 large eggs, lightly beaten

FOR THE WHIPPED CREAM

2 cups (16 fl oz/500 ml) heavy (double) cream

Sugar and brandy to taste

Makes 16 servings

NECTARINE FRANGIPANE TART

In midsummer in Northern California, every stone fruit seems to come off the trees at once: white peaches, blushing golden nectarines, and juicy plums of a dozen varieties can vie for the shopper's eye. When the harvest peaks, even reluctant Bay Area cooks get out their aprons, dust off their tart or pie recipes, and get to work. This luscious tart, filled with nectarines nesting in an almond paste cream, can just as successfully be made with peaches, figs, or plums. Frangipane is a sweet, creamy filling that always includes almonds and sometimes rum. If your tart pan is black, not silver, reduce the oven temperature to 375°F (190°C).

FOR THE DOUGH

1 cup (5 oz/155 g) unbleached all-purpose (plain) flour, plus more for dusting

1 tablespoon sugar

¼ teaspoon fine sea salt

½ cup (4 oz/125 g) chilled unsalted butter, cut into small pieces

1½ tablespoons ice water

FOR THE FILLING

4 tablespoons (2 oz/60 g) unsalted butter, at room temperature

4 oz (125 g) almond paste

⅓ cup (2 oz/60 g) all-purpose (plain) flour

1 large egg

FOR THE TOPPING

3 nectarines, about 1¼ lb (625 g) total weight, peeled, pitted, and cut into slices ¼–⅓ inch (6–9 mm) thick

1 tablespoon sugar

1 tablespoon unsalted butter, melted

⅓ cup (3 oz/90 g) peach or apricot jam

Makes one 9-inch (23-cm) tart, or 8 servings

1 To make the dough, in a food processor, combine the 1 cup flour, sugar, and salt. Pulse 3 or 4 times to blend. Add the butter and pulse until the mixture resembles coarse crumbs. Sprinkle the ice water over the mixture and pulse until the mixture just starts to clump. It will be crumbly but will hold together when pressed. Transfer the dough to a sheet of plastic wrap and shape it into a disk ¾ inch (2 cm) thick. Wrap tightly in the plastic wrap and refrigerate for 1 hour.

2 Remove the dough disk from the refrigerator and let stand for 10 minutes to soften. Unwrap the disk and put it on a work surface between 2 sheets of parchment (baking) paper each at least 10 inches (25 cm) square. Roll out the dough into an evenly thick round large enough to cover the bottom and sides of a 9-inch (23-cm) tart pan with a removable bottom. It should be about 10 inches (25 cm) in diameter. Flour the dough lightly as needed to keep it from sticking.

3 Peel off the top sheet of parchment, then invert the dough round into the tart pan, lift off the remaining parchment, and press the dough into place. Patch any thin spots with overhanging dough, although you should have little or no extra dough. If there is an overhang, roll the rolling pin across the rim of the pan to detach it. Cover with aluminum foil and freeze for 30 minutes.

4 Preheat the oven to 400°F (200°C). Line the tart shell with aluminum foil, covering the bottom and overhanging the sides. Fill the shell with dried beans or pie weights, covering the bottom evenly. Fold the edges of the foil loosely over the rim to protect it.

5 Bake the tart shell for 20 minutes, then carefully remove the beans and foil. With a fork, prick the bottom of the tart shell in several places. Continue baking the tart shell until it is lightly and evenly browned, 10–15 minutes longer. Transfer to a rack and let cool completely. Keep the oven set at 400°F.

6 To make the filling, in a stand mixer fitted with the paddle attachment or with a handheld mixer, combine the butter, almond paste, and flour. Beat on medium-low speed until completely smooth. Add the egg and beat at medium speed until creamy.

7 To make the topping, in a bowl, toss the nectarines with the sugar, coating them evenly.

8 To assemble the tart, spread the filling evenly in the cooled tart shell. Arrange the nectarine slices over the filling, starting at the edge and placing the slices close together in a ring. Fill the middle of the ring with more nectarine slices. You may not need all the slices. Brush the nectarines with the melted butter. Set the tart on a baking sheet and bake until the fruit is tender and the filling is puffed and firm, 30–35 minutes. Transfer to a rack and let cool for 15 minutes.

9 Just before the tart has finished cooling, in a small saucepan over low heat, melt the jam, then pass it through a medium-mesh sieve into a bowl. Thin it with water to a brushing consistency, then brush the nectarine slices. Serve the tart warm.

Serve with a rich, golden late-harvest dessert wine such as Riesling or Sauvignon Blanc or a French Sauternes.

MEYER LEMON POTS DE CRÈME WITH RASPBERRY SAUCE

Bay Area chefs can be wildly inventive when flavoring pots de crème, *the silky baked custards served in small pots. Ginger, bittersweet chocolate, dulce de leche (milk-based caramel), and espresso are among the* pot de crème *flavors that turn up on menus, but Meyer lemon—the fragrant citrus that thrives in local backyards—is perhaps the most inviting. Achieving a velvety texture with* pots de crème *takes some attention. If you overcook them, they will be overly firm once chilled. Make sure they are still quivery when you remove them from the oven.*

1 Preheat the oven to 300°F (150°C) degrees. In a small nonreactive saucepan over medium-low heat, combine the cream, milk, granulated sugar, salt, and lemon zest and bring slowly to a simmer. In a bowl, whisk the egg yolks until blended. Gradually add the hot cream mixture to the egg yolks, whisking constantly. Pour through a fine-mesh sieve into a 1-qt (1-l) measuring pitcher, and press on the zest with a rubber spatula to extract the flavor.

2 Place six ¾-cup (6–fl oz/180-ml) custard cups in a baking dish just large enough to hold them without touching. Divide the custard mixture evenly among the cups. Carefully pour boiling water into the baking dish to come halfway up the sides of the cups. Cover the baking dish with aluminum foil. Bake the custards until barely set, 35–37 minutes. They should still jiggle a little in the center; they will firm as they cool.

3 Remove the cups from the water bath and let cool completely on a rack, then cover and refrigerate until well chilled, about 8 hours.

4 To make the sauce, in a food processor, combine the raspberries and sugar and process until smooth. Pass through a fine-mesh sieve into a bowl, pressing firmly on the solids with a rubber spatula. Cover and refrigerate until chilled, about 4 hours.

5 About 30 minutes before serving, remove the *pots de crème* from the refrigerator. Pass the chilled raspberry sauce separately.

Serve with a late-harvest dessert wine such as Muscat.

1½ cups (12 fl oz/375 ml) heavy (double) cream

1 cup (8 fl oz/250 ml) whole milk

⅓ cup (3 oz/90 g) granulated sugar

Pinch of fine sea salt

3 tablespoons grated Meyer lemon zest (from about 4 large lemons)

8 large egg yolks

FOR THE SAUCE

¾ cup (3 oz/90 g) raspberries

2 teaspoons superfine (caster) sugar

Makes 6 servings

Meyer Lemons

More fragrant, sweeter, and juicier than the familiar Eureka and Lisbon lemons, the Meyer lemon is a Bay Area darling. Thought to be a cross between a lemon and either a mandarin or an orange, the Meyer turns golden when ripe. The flesh is yellow-gold with a floral perfume.

For years, the Meyer lemon was primarily a backyard fruit in the Bay Area. But in the 1980s, Chez Panisse pastry chef Lindsey Shere began to work with the aromatic citrus, and word of her luscious Meyer lemon desserts—tarts, ice cream, and custards—began to spread. To satisfy the growing demand, several California growers established commercial plantings of Meyer lemons. Today, Meyers are relatively plentiful in specialty produce markets during the winter, and even more widespread in home landscapes.

Bay Area cooks use Meyer lemon juice in salad dressings, lemonade, cocktails, and desserts. The freshly grated zest adds fragrance to muffins and cakes. A local distillery makes a popular Meyer lemon vodka, and at least one Bay Area olive oil producer crushes olives with Meyer lemons to make a fragrant oil for use as a condiment.

SOFT-CENTERED CHOCOLATE CAKE WITH ESPRESSO ICE CREAM

Soft-centered chocolate cakes are popular across the country, but San Francisco cooks can boast of making the dessert with local chocolate—from Ghirardelli, Guittard, or Scharffen Berger. Take care not to overcook these individual cakes, and serve them promptly or they will lose their characteristic moist center. Because all ovens don't bake evenly, you may want to conduct a test run so that you know exactly how long it takes to bake the cakes to perfection in your oven. Homemade espresso ice cream is an impressive accompaniment, but you can always substitute store-bought ice cream or other flavors such as vanilla or pistachio.

FOR THE ICE CREAM

1 cup (8 fl oz/250 ml) heavy (double) cream

1 cup (8 fl oz/250 ml) half-and-half (half cream)

1 tablespoon instant espresso powder

¼ vanilla bean, split lengthwise

4 large egg yolks

½ cup (4 oz/125 g) sugar

FOR THE CAKE

⅔ cup (5 oz/155 g) unsalted butter

5 oz (155 g) top-quality bittersweet chocolate, chopped

2 large whole eggs plus 1 large egg white

¾ cup (6 oz/185 g) sugar

½ cup (2 oz/60 g) sifted all-purpose (plain) flour

Makes 4 servings

1 To make the ice cream, in a saucepan, combine the cream, half-and-half, and espresso. Using the tip of a knife, scrape the vanilla seeds from the pod halves into the milk, then add the pod halves. Whisk to blend, place over medium-low heat, bring to a simmer, cover, remove from the heat, and let steep for 15 minutes.

2 In a bowl, whisk together the egg yolks and sugar until the mixture is pale yellow and forms a ribbon when the whisk is lifted. This should take about 3 minutes. Gradually whisk in the hot cream mixture (including the vanilla pod). Return the mixture to the saucepan and cook over medium-low heat, stirring constantly with a wooden spoon, until the mixture visibly thickens and coats the spoon. (It should register 178°F/81°C on an instant-read thermometer.) Do not let it boil, or it will curdle.

3 Immediately remove the custard from the heat and continue stirring for 1 minute. Pour through a fine-mesh sieve into a bowl. Let the custard cool, cover, and refrigerate until well chilled, about 8 hours or up to overnight. Freeze in an ice-cream maker according to the manufacturer's directions. Transfer to an airtight container and place in the freezer.

4 To make the cake, preheat the oven to 350°F (180°C). Butter the bottoms and sides of four 1-cup (8–fl oz/250-ml) ramekins. Dust with flour, then tap out the excess.

5 In a small saucepan over medium-low heat, melt the butter. Remove from the heat and add the chocolate. Let stand until the chocolate softens, then stir until smooth.

6 In a bowl, whisk together the whole eggs, egg white, and sugar until well blended. Add the chocolate mixture and incorporate thoroughly. Gently fold in the flour. Divide among the prepared ramekins, then place the ramekins on a baking sheet.

7 Bake the cakes until they are puffed and cracked on top, 26–28 minutes. Remove from the oven and, working with 1 cake at a time, gently invert onto a dessert plate. Turn right side up, let cool for about 3 minutes, and then serve with the ice cream.

GLOSSARY

ALMOND PASTE A mixture of ground blanched almonds, sugar, and liquid glucose used in the making of candies, cakes, and other desserts. Look for it in packaged cylinders—it should be malleable to the touch—in the baking section of supermarkets.

ANCHOVY This small fish is most commonly available cured, either as fillets packed in oil or whole fish packed in salt. The latter must be filleted and rinsed before use.

ANISE LIQUEUR A strongly flavored distilled spirit made from green aniseeds, anise liqueur is produced under different names in a number of countries, including Pernod in France, anesone and sambuca in Italy, raki in Turkey, and ouzo in Greece. French pastis is a similar liqueur that is based on licorice instead of anise.

ARTICHOKE The flower bud of a plant belonging to the thistle family, the artichoke comes both large and small. So-called baby artichokes are not immature specimens, but the smaller buds that grow near the base of the plant. A favorite of San Francisco's Italian Americans, the prickly vegetable is cultivated in coastal fields south of San Francisco. The main season is in early spring, followed by a second, shorter season in late fall.

ARUGULA Also known as rocket, this peppery green has sword-shaped, deeply notched leaves 2 to 3 inches (5 to 7.5 cm) long. Sold in small bunches or prewashed loose leaves, it adds a spicy note to salads, may be cooked in pasta sauces, and tops pizzas.

ASIAN SESAME OIL A fragrant, deep amber oil made by extracting oil from roasted sesame seeds. Used primarily in Japan, Korea, and China, where it is employed as a flavoring rather than a cooking oil.

BALSAMIC VINEGAR The celebrated vinegar of Modena, in Emilia-Romagna, is made by aging pure wine must (unfermented grape juice) in wooden barrels for anywhere from 1 year to more than 75 years. Younger vinegars are used for salad dressings and glazes, while more costly, syrupy, long-aged vinegars are used in tiny amounts as an intense flavoring.

BASIL, ITALIAN AND THAI Although related to mint, basil tastes of anise and cloves. Italian, or sweet, basil has robust, deep green, furrowed leaves, while Thai basil, a tropical variety of sweet basil, has small green leaves, purple stems and flowers, and a more pronounced anise taste.

BEET Also called beetroots, beets are most commonly dark red, but farmers' markets and well-stocked produce departments carry golden, pink, and white varieties, as well as the pink-and-white-striped Chioggia beet. Although available year-round, beets are at their best in late summer and autumn and can be as small as a lime or as large as a small orange. To ensure freshness, buy beets with their greens—which should show no signs of browning—and 1 to 2 inches (2.5 to 5 cm) of their roots intact, then, once home, cut off the greens and store beets and greens separately.

BLOOD ORANGE These dramatic fruits are originally from Sicily. Their distinctive flesh ranges from a light blush to a deep, rich red, and they have a berrylike flavor. Because of their versatility, blood oranges are a favorite winter fruit of Bay Area chefs.

BROCCOLI RABE Also known as broccoli raab, *cime di rapa,* and rapini, this pleasantly bitter member of the cabbage family has long, thin stalks, ending in florets; the leaves are slender and jagged edged. Look for it in wintertime.

CANNELLINI BEAN Dried, white kidney-shaped bean used in Italian dishes. Great Northern beans may be substituted.

CAPER The small unopened flower buds of a Mediterranean shrub, capers are dried and packed in brine or salt. Brined capers are sold in jars; salted capers are available in bulk or in jars in specialty markets. Always rinse the latter before use.

CHILES The Bay Area's sizable Latino and Asian populations have put fresh and dried chiles in most local food markets. To prevent burns, wear rubber gloves when working with hot chiles, and avoid touching your eyes, mouth, or other sensitive areas. Wash your hands and utensils in hot, soapy water promptly after finishing.

CHIPOTLE Smoked and dried jalapeños, chipotles are moderately hot and have a smoky flavor. They are most commonly available canned in adobo sauce, a blend of garlic, tomatoes, and vinegar.

SERRANO A slender, shiny fresh red or green chile about 3 inches (7.5 cm) long and very hot.

POBLANO These black-green, triangular-shaped fresh chiles are about 5 inches (13 cm) long and are moderately hot.

THAI Small, thin, extremely hot green or red fresh chiles, usually about 1 inch (2.5 cm) long. Also known as bird chiles.

CHORIZO, MEXICAN This fresh pork sausage, sold in links, is typically spicier than its smoked Spanish cousin. Mexican chorizos are sold in the refrigerator case of Latino markets and many supermarkets.

CILANTRO The green, finely notched leaves of this pungent herb resemble those of Italian (flat-leaf) parsley. Also known as fresh coriander or Chinese parsley, cilantro is used in Latin American, Middle Eastern, and Asian cuisines.

CREMA A thick, rich, slightly soured Mexican cream made at home or found in grocery stores. Homemade crème fraîche (see below), or commercial crème fraîche or sour cream thinned slightly with milk can be substituted.

CRÈME FRAÎCHE This soured, cultured French cream is similar to sour cream; unlike sour cream, however, it will not separate when added to hot foods and it can be whipped. Look for it in the dairy section of markets, or make your own: Stir 2 tablespoons buttermilk into 1 cup (8 fl oz/250 ml) heavy (double) cream in a plastic or glass container. Cover tightly and let stand in a warm spot, shaking once or twice, until thickened, 24 to 48 hours. Stir and use immediately, or cover and refrigerate for up to 1 week.

ESCAROLE The sturdy, slightly ruffled, mildly bitter leaves of this chicory relative are used both raw and cooked. The leaves at the heart of the head are usually a creamy yellow, while the outer leaves are a bright green. Escarole is available year-round but is best in winter.

FAVA BEANS Also called broad beans or horse beans, this shell bean is available fresh in spring and early summer. Once shelled, the beans should be peeled of their tough outer skin unless they are very young and tender. To peel, blanch the shelled beans briefly in boiling water, shock in ice water, then pinch the beans to remove the skins.

FENNEL Also known as sweet fennel or finocchio, fennel's bulb, stems, and fronds have a sweet, aniselike flavor and can be eaten raw or cooked. Choose fat, rounded white to pale green bulbs that are smooth and tightly layered, with no cracks or bruises. Avoid any with wilted leaves or dry layers. Available year-round, fennel is at its peak from late fall through winter.

FISH SAUCE Made by layering anchovies or other tiny fish with salt in barrels or jars and leaving them to ferment, this dark amber liquid adds its pungent, salty flavor to many Southeast Asian dishes. Thai *nam pla* and Vietnamese *nuoc mam* fish sauces are the most readily available types.

FIVE-SPICE POWDER Used primarily in kitchens in southern China and Vietnam, this seasoning mixture, not always made up of five spices, typically includes star anise, cassia (a type of cinnamon), fennel, cloves, Sichuan peppercorns, and sometimes ginger and/or cardamom.

FOCACCIA See page 39.

FRISÉE Curly-leaved member of the chicory family, frisée comes in small heads with ivory yellow, lacy leaves at the heart surrounded by larger pale green leaves. Its crisp texture and slightly bitter flavor are prized in salads. Available year-round, frisée is at its best in spring and fall.

GALANGAL Similar in appearance to its relative, ginger, galangal is a pale yellow, striped rhizome with pink shoots. Its peppery flavor is appreciated in many Southeast Asian dishes, especially in Thailand and Indonesia. Fresh galangal is found in Southeast Asian markets and some produce markets.

JUNIPER BERRY The small, blue-black berries of the juniper shrub, indispensable in the manufacture of gin, lend a pungent, bittersweet flavor to marinades and other preparations. They are widely sold in the spice section of food stores.

KAFFIR LIME LEAVES Also called makrut lime; see page 62.

LENTIL Small and disk shaped, this dried legume is mild flavored and quick cooking. Lentils come in a variety of colors, from yellow and red to brown, green, and black. Bay Area chefs particularly prize tiny green French lentils, called lentilles de Puy.

LONG BEAN, CHINESE See page 62.

MASCARPONE A soft, rich, smooth fresh Italian dairy product made from cream, mascarpone is sold in plastic tubs in the cheese section of Italian markets and fine food stores. It is used both in savory and sweet dishes.

MEYER LEMON See page 181.

MUSSEL This saltwater mollusk has a slightly pointed shell and cream- or orange-colored meat that is usually sweeter than that of oysters or clams. Most mussels available commercially are cultivated. The Atlantic blue, or common, mussel, which is actually quite black, is 2 to 3 inches (5 to 7.5 cm) long. Buy only live mussels, which will have a fresh sea smell and will close when tapped. Store in a bowl, covered with a damp kitchen towel, in the refrigerator, for up to 24 hours.

SCRUBBING AND DEBEARDING MUSSELS: Scrub grit off the shells with a stiff-bristled brush. Just before cooking, remove any beard (the tuft of fibers the mussel uses to connect to rocks or pilings) by cutting and scraping it with a knife or scissors. (Many farm-raised mussels today have little or no beard.) Live mussels will open when cooked. Discard any that remain closed.

OLALLIEBERRY Plump, juicy blackberry hybrid grown in California, olallieberries are not usually available outside the state. They are found primarily at farmers' markets or at pick-your-own farms.

OLIVE OIL See page 151.

OLIVES, PICHOLINE AND NIÇOISE Picholine olives, which grow in southern France, are plump, medium-green, firm fruits with pointed ends. they have a mellow flavor. Niçoise olives, also from southern France, are tiny, purplish black, and fleshy and have a rich flavor.

ORECCHIETTE The name of this small, circular pasta, with a hollow at the center, translates as "little ears." Most widely available dried, orecchiette is often paired with broccoli rabe or tomato sauce.

PANCETTA A spiced and cured, but not smoked, Italian bacon, pancetta derives its name from the Italian word for "belly." It is made by rubbing a slab of pork belly with a mixture of spices, then rolling it into a tight cylinder and curing for at least 2 months. It has a moist, silky texture and is typically sold in thin slices in butcher shops and Italian delicatessens.

PARMIGIANO-REGGIANO CHEESE An aged, firm cheese with a piquant, slightly salty taste, authentic Italian Parmigiano-Reggiano is produced in the Emilia-Romagna region under stringent standards. It is made in enormous, shiny golden wheels that, when split open, reveal a straw yellow, grainy interior. Parmigiano-Reggiano is largely used as a fine grating cheese but it also makes an excellent table cheese.

PERSIMMON, HACHIYA The larger of the two kinds of persimmons available in food markets (the other is the Fuyu), the deep orange Hachiya is shaped like an acorn. It is eaten when ripe and very soft to the touch; otherwise, it is extremely astringent. Ripen firm fruits at room temperature; ripe fruits may be refrigerated for up to 3 days. To prepare, remove the stem, halve and remove any black seeds, then spoon the flesh from the peel.

POLENTA Polenta is cornmeal cooked in a generous amount of liquid until it thickens and the grains are tender. In Italy, polenta may be yellow or white, coarsely or finely ground, but the classic version is made from coarsely ground yellow corn.

PORCINI MUSHROOMS Also known as ceps or boletes, porcini are plump, firm wild mushrooms with a rich, earthy flavor. Fresh porcini are available in winter in some gourmet produce markets. Intensely flavored dried porcini are available year-round; to use, soak them in hot water for about 30 minutes to rehydrate.

RADICCHIO A variety of chicory native to Italy, radicchio may be eaten cooked or raw. The most common types grown in the United States are the round Verona and the elongated Treviso. The variegated purple-red leaves are sturdy and moderately bitter.

RICOTTA See page 68.

RICOTTA SALATA A mild, white, lightly salted Italian sheep's milk cheese that has been aged for about 3 months. It is similar to Greek mizithra and can be shaved or grated.

SAFFRON The stigmas of a Mediterranean crocus, saffron is pungent and earthy, with a slightly medicinal flavor. It is considered the world's most expensive spice. Saffron is available in two forms, threads or powdered. The threads are more commonly used and are usually soaked in a small amount of hot liquid, imparting its characteristic deep yellow color to the soaking liquid, before adding to any dish.

SALMON ROE The bright orange-red, glistening eggs of salmon are valued for their color, salty taste, and slightly crunchy texture. The roe is available fresh, pasteurized, or frozen and should be eaten promptly after opening or thawing.

SALT, SEA AND KOSHER Naturally evaporated sea salt is available in coarse or fine grains. Sea salt has more flavor than table salt, thanks to its mineral content, and is often preferred by chefs. Kosher salt generally contains no additives, has large flakes and is superior in flavor to table salt.

SEMOLINA This lightly gritty, golden flour is milled from high-protein durum wheat. Semolina is used to make the highest-quality dried pasta and in some pizza doughs and breads. Look for semolina in Italian markets.

SHRIMP Ranging in size from tiny to extra colossal, shrimp (prawns) are saltwater shellfish that are gray when raw and pink when cooked. They may be cooked with or without their shells, and deveined before or after cooking.

PEELING SHRIMP: If the head is intact, pull it off. Carefully pull off the legs on the inside curve of the body and peel off the shell, removing the tail as well, unless the recipe specifies otherwise.

DEVEINING SHRIMP: With a small knife, cut a shallow groove along the back of a peeled shrimp. With the tip of the knife, gently lift out the dark vein.

TELEME CHEESE See page 68.

THAI ROASTED CHILE PASTE Dried red chiles, garlic, and shallots, all roasted to bring out their flavor, are mixed with oil to make this fiery condiment, known as *nahm prik pao* in Thai. Used to flavor stir-fries, soups, and fried rice dishes, it is sold in jars in Asian markets.

TOMATILLO Resembling a small green tomato, this member of the gooseberry family has a citruslike flavor and a firm texture, and is used in fresh and cooked salsas and in stews. Fresh tomatillos are available in Latino markets and some produce markets year-round, but are at their peak in late fall. Remove the parchmentlike husk and rinse away the natural sticky coating before using.

TOMATO Tomatoes are generally available in three types, round, plum, and cherry. Medium- or large-sized round tomatoes are excellent for slicing, while egg-shaped plum, or Roma, varieties have more pulp and less juice, making them perfect for sauces. Small cherry tomatoes are available in a variety of colors and shapes. For information on heirloom tomatoes, see page 117.

PEELING AND SEEDING TOMATOES: Cut a shallow X in the blossom end of the tomato. Immerse in a pan of boiling water until the peel begins to curl away from the X, about 30 seconds. Transfer to a bowl of ice water to cool, then peel away the skin. To seed, cut in half crosswise and squeeze each half gently to dislodge the seeds.

VANILLA Vanilla is available as whole beans or as bottled extract (essence). If using extract, look for a product labeled "pure vanilla extract." Choose pliable, moist beans with a white "bloom." If a recipe calls for the seeds, split the bean in half lengthwise with a paring knife, then, using the tip of the knife, scrape out the seeds from the inside of each pod half. Some recipes call for adding the flavorful pod halves as well.

WATER CHESTNUTS Fresh water chestnuts, walnut-sized, dark brown corms, are grown in ponds, streams, and rivers. Their white flesh is sweet, slightly starchy, and crunchy. Look for fresh water chestnuts in Asian markets, and rinse well and peel before using. Rinse more widely available canned peeled water chestnuts before using.

INDEX

ACKNOWLEDGMENTS

Janet Fletcher would like to acknowledge Wendy Weiden's considerable and conscientious help with recipe testing and thank Hannah Rahill, Kim Goodfriend, and Heather Belt from Weldon Owen for being so consistently accommodating and good-natured, and for inviting her to participate in this gratifying project.

Jean-Blaise Hall would like to thank his photo assistants Brooke Buchanan and Adam Aronson; Stuart and Jacqueline Schwartz for their great hospitality; and Birte Walter.

Weldon Owen wishes to thank the following individuals and organizations for their kind assistance: Desne Ahlers, Dan Becker, Ken DellaPenta, Signe Jensen, Karen Kemp, Joan Olson, Scott Panton, Eric Ryan, Sharon Silva, and Karin Skaggs.

Weldon Owen would also like to extend their gratitude to the owners and workers of restaurants, bakeries, shops, and other culinary businesses in San Francisco and the Bay Area who participated in this project: Absinthe Brasserie and Bar, Steve Sullivan of Acme Bread Company, Johnny Alamilla of Alma, Debbie Zachareas of Bacar, Bar-Or Ranch, Michael Wild of Bay Wolf, Beach Chalet, Boudin Bakery, Bryan's Market, Café Fanny, Café La Haye, Caffe Roma, Caffe Trieste, Cheese Board, Chimney Rock Winery, CIA Greystone, Citizen Cake, Christopher Rossi of Citron, Cowgirl Creamery, Delfina Restaurant, Domaine Carneros, Fog City Diner, French Laundry, Ghirardelli Chocolate Shop and Caffe, Gordon's, Graffeo Coffee Roasting Company, Jeff Dodge of La Farine Bakery, La Palma Mexicatessen, La Taqueria, Mario's Bohemian Cigar Store and Café, Molinari Deli, Monterey Fish, Mustards, North Berkeley Imports, Pasta Shop, Real Foods, Roosevelt Tamale Parlor, San Francisco Brewing Company, Scharffen Berger, Schramsberg, SF Alemany Farmers' Market, SF Civic Center Farmers' Market, SF Ferry Plaza Farmers' Market, Swan Oyster Depot, Mary Risley of Tante Marie's Cooking School, Tartine Bakery, Toronado Bar, Tosca, Vella Cheese Company, Ver Brugge Meats, Yank Sing, and Judy Rodgers of Zuni.

PHOTO CREDITS

Jean-Blaise Hall, all photography, except for the following:
Quentin Bacon. Pages 78, 80–81
Lauren Burke: Pages 11 (upper right), 12 (upper left), 13 (center), 14 (center), 19 (upper right), 21, 28 (center), 36–37, 51 (upper right), 71 (upper right, lower right, lower right center), 84, 90, 121 (upper right, lower left), 129, 135, 140, 152, 156, 161, 162, 167 (upper right), 173
Sheri Giblin: Pages 38–39, 42–43, 46–47, 52–53, 58–59, 62–63, 68–69
Jeremy Woodhouse: Cover (upper image)

PHOTOGRAPHY LOCATIONS

The following San Francisco and Bay Area locations have been given references for the map on pages 30–31.

Oxmoor
House.

OXMOOR HOUSE, INC.

Oxmoor House books are distributed by Sunset Books
80 Willow Road, Menlo Park, CA 94025
Telephone: 650-321-3600 Fax: 650-324-1532
Vice President/General Manager Rich Smeby
National Accounts Manager/Special Sales Brad Moses
Oxmoor House and Sunset Books are divisions of
Southern Progress Corporation

WILLIAMS-SONOMA, INC.

Founder & Vice-Chairman Chuck Williams

THE FOODS OF THE WORLD SERIES

Conceived and produced by Weldon Owen Inc.
814 Montgomery Street, San Francisco, CA 94133
Telephone: 415-291-0100 Fax: 415-291-8841

In Collaboration with Williams-Sonoma, Inc.
3250 Van Ness Avenue, San Francisco, CA 94109

A Weldon Owen Production
Copyright © 2004 Weldon Owen Inc.
and Williams-Sonoma, Inc.

All rights reserved, including the right of
reproduction in whole or in part in any form.

Foods of the World is a trademark of Oxmoor House, Inc.

First printed in 2004
10 9 8 7 6 5 4 3 2 1

ISBN 0-8487-2852-1

Printed by Tien Wah Press
Printed in Singapore

WELDON OWEN INC.

Chief Executive Officer John Owen
President and Chief Operating Officer Terry Newell
Vice President International Sales Stuart Laurence
Creative Director Gaye Allen
Publisher Hannah Rahill
Business Manager Richard Van Oosterhout

Series Editor Kim Goodfriend
Editor Heather Belt
Assistant Editor Donita Boles
Editorial Assistant Juli Vendzules

Associate Creative Director Leslie Harrington
Art Director Nicky Collings
Designers Teri Gardiner, Marisa Kwek
Map Illustrator Scott Panton
Photo Researcher Liz Lazich

Production Director Chris Hemesath
Color Specialist Teri Bell
Production and Shipping Coordinator Todd Rechner

Food Stylist George Dolese
Prop Stylist Sara Slavin
Associate Food Stylist Elisabet der Nederlanden
Photographer's Assistants Brooke Buchanan,
Adam Aronson

A NOTE ON WEIGHTS AND MEASURES

All recipes include customary U.S. and metric
measurements. Metric conversions are based on
a standard developed for these books and have
been rounded off. Actual weights may vary.